LEXIPRO

ANGLAIS

Les mots clés du droit

Classement thématique

Exemples d'utilisation

Index bilingue

Frédérique CORBIÈRE-LÉVY
Professeur agrégé
Université de Rouen

Bréal

ISBN : 9782749534091

Impression & brochage SEPEC - France
Numéro d'impression : 10803150206 - Dépôt légal : février 2015

PEFC™ 10-31-1470 / Certifié PEFC / Ce produit est issu de forêts gérées durablement et de sources contrôlées. / pefc-france.org

SOMMAIRE

AVANT-PROPOS

L'internationalisation des marchés s'effectue sous la domination de la langue anglo-américaine. Elle implique donc, pour les juristes comme pour l'ensemble des gestionnaires et administrateurs francophones, la capacité de passer aisément dans le cadre de leur champ professionnel d'une langue technique à une autre. Pour répondre à ces besoins, ce lexique propose en 9 chapitres correspondant aux différentes branches du droit une sélection de mots français traduits en anglais.
Cet ouvrage s'adresse aux élèves des écoles de commerce ainsi qu'aux étudiants des UFR de sciences juridiques, de sciences économiques, AES, LEA, Licences professionnelles, sans oublier ceux des filières tertiaires des sections de techniciens supérieurs et des IUT. Il est également destiné aux praticiens du droit (avocats, juristes d'entreprise…).
Ainsi, étudiants et professionnels seront mieux en mesure de faire face aux problèmes lexicaux que pose l'étude des différentes branches du droit anglais.

L'auteur

LE PERSONNEL JUDICIAIRE, LES TRIBUNAUX, LA POLICE

THE PERSONNEL OF THE LAW, COURTS OF LAW, THE POLICE

aide judiciaire
legal aid
Legal aid concerns the provisions of free legal service.

associer à (s')
become a partner (to)
A solicitor may become a partner with other solicitors and form a partnership.

avocat
solicitor (GB)
Solicitors undertake the general aspects of giving legal advice and conducting legal proceedings.

barrister (GB)
A barrister is a legal practitioner admitted to plead at the Bar.

advocate
An advocate is someone who argues a case for a client in court.

counsel
A counsel is a lawyer who gives advice on a legal case and fights the case in court.

lawyer (US) / attorney (US)

avocat commis d'office
duty solicitor
A duty solicitor provides immediate advice and assistance for someone who is appearing before Magistrates' Courts and is unassisted.

avocat de la Couronne
Queen's counsel / QC
When a barrister decides to become a Queen's counsel / QC, he decides to "take silk".

avocat de la défense
defending counsel

avocat de la partie civile
prosecuting counsel

barreau
Bar
The Bar means barristers collectively.

> **être inscrit au barreau**
> to be called to the Bar (GB) / to be admitted to the Bar (US)
> *To be called to the Bar is to be admitted to the profession by one of the Inns of Court.*

> **préparer le barreau**
> to read for the Bar

cabinet juridique
law firm
There are about 7,000 law firms in Great Britain nowadays.

Chambre du Banc de la Reine
Queen's Bench Division
The Queen's Bench Division is one of the divisions of the High Court.

chef du parquet
Director of Public Prosecution / DPP
The Director of Public Prosecution / DPP is appointed by the Home Secretary, he is head of the National Crown Prosecution Service.

client
client
An advocate argues cases for clients in court.

conseil du barreau
Bar Council (the)
The Bar Council was formerly called the Bar Committee.

> **être radié du barreau**
> be disbarred (to)
> *If a barrister has not been briefed by a solicitor and goes to court he can be disbarred.*

> **radiation du barreau**
> disbarment

> **rayer de l'ordre des *solicitors***
> be struck off from the Roll of Solicitors (to)
> *A solicitor may be struck off from the Roll of Solicitors according to the Solicitors Act 1974.*

conseil de prud'hommes
Industrial Tribunal
An Industrial Tribunal settles the principal problems which may arise between employer and employee.

cooptation
co-option
Benchers are not elected but chosen by co-option.

« **coroner** »
coroner
The coroner is a public official who investigates sudden violent deaths.

cour
court
Divorce courts.

> **la Cour (formation des magistrats qui y siègent)**
> the Bench

cour d'appel
Court of Appeal
The Court of Appeal is divided into two divisions: the Civil Division and Criminal Division.

cour d'appel fédérale
Court of Appeals (US)

cour de comté
County Court
A County Court hears most civil cases where the sum of money is low.

cour de district / de circuit
District / Circuit Court

Cour européenne de justice
European Court of Justice
The European Court of Justice deals with European law matters.

cour martiale
court martial
A court martial has jurisdiction when the offences are committed by a member of the Armed Forces.

Cour suprême
Supreme Court (US)
An important function of the Supreme Court is to exercice the power of judicial review.

docteur en droit
Doctor of Laws / LD

droit
law
A Law student.

droit administratif
administrative law

droit basé sur le droit jurisprudentiel
common law

droit civil
civil law

droit commercial
commercial law

droit de la consommation
consumer law

droit de la famille
family law

droit de la responsabilité (quasi délictuelle)
law of tort

droit en vigueur dans le pays
law of the land

droit des contrats
contract law

droit des sociétés
company law

droit fiscal
Revenue law

droit pénal
criminal law / crime law

droit public
public law

droit (point de)
point of law

droit (question de)
issue / question of law

écoles de droit (à Londres)
Inns of Court (the)
There are four Inns of Court: Inner Temple, Middle Temple, Gray's Inn and Lincoln's Inn.

émoluments (avoué)
solicitor's charges

en exercice
practising
A practising barrister.

exercer
practise (to)
This barrister has been practising for over ten years.

formation plénière (en)
in a full court

frais de justice
court costs / court fees
High Court costs / fees are said to be a powerful incentive to out of court settlement.

greffe
registry office

greffier
registrar
The registrar keeps records and can hear preliminary arguments in civil cases.

Haute Cour de justice
High Court of Justice
The High Court of Justice is divided into three divisions: the Queen's Bench Division, Chancery Division and Family Division.

honoraires
fees
The client questioned the amount of the fees he had to pay.

huissier
bailiff
A bailiff is a law officer who makes sure that the decisions of a court are obeyed.

inamovible
irremovable
Puisne judges are irremovable.

jour d'audience
court day

judiciaire
judicial
A judicial assembly.

> **l'autorité judiciaire**
> the judiciary
> *The judiciary is concerned with justice and the legal system.*

juge
judge
Last week he appeared before the judge.

juge à temps partiel
recorder / lay magistrate
Recorders / Lay magistrates are appointed on a temporary basis.

juge de « circuit »
circuit judge
Circuit judges have no fixity of tenure and are not irremovable.

juge d'instruction
examining justice

juge de la Chambre des Lords
Lord of Appeal in Ordinary
A Lord of Appeal in Ordinary is a life peer.

juge de la cour d'appel
Lord Justice of Appeal

juge de la High Court of Justice
puisne judge / Justice of the High Court
When in court the Justice of the High Court / puisne judge is adressed as "Mr Justice".

juge de paix
Justice of the Peace / JP
The Justice of the Peace is a lay person.

juge de première instance
circuit judge of first instance

juge des référés
judge in chambers

juge du fond
trial judge

juger
try (to)
Offences such as murder, treason, etc. must be tried by a High Court Judge.

juré
juror
Each juror must swear that he / she will faith-fully try the case and give a true verdict according to the evidence.

faire partie des juridictions supérieures
fixity of tenure (to have)
Circuit judges have no fixity of tenure and are not irremovable.

juridique
legal
The government is keen to introduce competition on the legal services market.

juriste
lawyer
Solicitors and barristers are both lawyers.

jury
jury
The verdict of the jury should, if possible, be unanimous.

> **constituer un jury**
> to empanel a jury

> **exercer la fonction de jury**
> to do jury service

> **président du jury**
> foreman jury
> *The foreman jury is the leader of the jury, he is the one who pronounces the verdict in court.*

licence en droit
law degree / LLB
Applications are invited from holders of a law degree / LLB.

> **licencié en droit**
> Bachelor of Laws

magistrature (la)
the Judiciary
The English Judiciary is made up of former barristers and solicitors.

mandat
warrant
Under the Theft Act 1968, police may obtain a warrant to search for stolen goods when there are reasonable grounds for believing that they are in someone's possession.

ministère public
Crown Prosecution Service
The Crown Prosecution Service is headed by the Director of Public Prosecution under the superintendence of the Attorney General.

ministre de la Justice
Lord Chancellor
The Lord Chancellor is head of the Judiciary.
Attorney General / AG (US)

non-juriste
lay
The Justices of the Peace are lay persons.

officier de justice de la Couronne
Law Officer of the Crown
There are two Law Officers of the Crown: the Attorney General and the Solicitor General.

officier de police
police officer
He has been a police officer for 10 years.

palais de justice
courthouse
A courthouse is a building in which a court of law meets.

parquet
Crown Prosecution Service
The Crown Prosecution Service was established in 1986.

police
police
Police and Criminal Evidence Act 1984.

> **agent de police**
> police constable
> *A police constable is a policeman of the lowest rank.*

> **commissaire de police**
> superintendent
> *A superintendent is someone who has a high rank in the police force.*

> **commissariat de police**
> police station
> *In England, fingerprints are taken at the police station.*

> **fonctionnaire de police**
> police officer
> *Have you met the new police officer?*

> **inspecteur de police**
> police inspector
> *The police inspector is questioning the suspect.*

> **préfet de police**
> Commissioner
> *"The Commissioner is not answering questions", said the journalist to his friend.*

président de la cour d'appel
Master of the Rolls
Lord Denning was Master of the Rolls until 1985.

procureur
prosecutor
A prosecutor is someone who institutes criminal proceedings on behalf of the Crown.

procureur général
Attorney General
The Attorney General is the English equivalent of the procureur général or the US equivalent of the garde des Sceaux.

révocable
removable
Recorders are removable by the Lord Chancellor.

salle d'audience
court room
A court room is a room in which a legal court meets.

service des affaires criminelles
Criminal Investigation Department
The Criminal Investigation Department is the police department in charge of investigating all criminal affairs.

session
term
A legal year is divided into four law terms.

stage (du solicitor)
articles
The period of on-the-job training that a solicitor must do before he can be fully qualified is called articles.

> **être en stage (chez un barrister)**
> to enter pupillage
> *After being called to the Bar, the barrister has to undergo a period of pupillage.*

> **être en stage (chez un solicitor)**
> to be articled / to serve a period of articles
> *Being articled to a solicitor is often called "sitting with Nelly".*

tribunal
court
Juvenile court.
tribunal
A tribunal is a special court that is appointed to deal with particular problems.

PROCÉDURES CIVILE ET PÉNALE

CIVIL AND CRIMINAL PROCEEDINGS

1

ACTIONS CIVILE ET PÉNALE
CIVIL AND CRIMINAL ACTIONS

accusation
charge
A murder charge.

> **porter une accusation contre qqn**
> to bring / to lay a charge against sb

acte d'accusation
indictment
An indictment is an official charge of a crime made against a person.

> **lecture de l'acte d'accusation**
> arraignment
> *Once the accused appears in court he is called to the bar and the first formal step of his trial is the arraignment.*

> **rédiger l'acte d'accusation**
> to draw up the indictment

> **sur mise en accusation**
> on indictment

accusé
defendant
The defendant is the person against whom the lawsuit has been brought.

action civile
civil action

action en contrefaçon
action for infringement of patent

action en cours
pending action
A pending lawsuit.

action en désaveu de paternité
action for disavowal

action en diffamation orale
action for slander

action en dommages et intérêts
action for damages

action en exécution de contrat
action for specific performance

action en expropriation
action in expropriation of real property

action en justice
action
He brought an action against the burglars.

action en résolution pour inexécution
action for breach of contract

action en séparation de corps
action for separation from bed and board

action par défaut
default action

action pénale
criminal action

affaire
case
The inspector on the case.

ajournement
adjournment
An adjournment was called.

> **proposer l'ajournement**
> to move the adjournment

à l'amiable
friendly / out of court / amicable
An out of court / friendly / amicable settlement.

alibi
alibi
An unassailable alibi.

allégation
allegation
It is the duty of the party who makes an allegation to adduce evidence in support of it at trial.

appel
appeal
If the appeal is allowed, the court may reverse the decision of the lower court, amend it or order a new trial.

> **d'appel**
> appellate
> *The jurisdiction of the House of Lords is almost entirely appellate.*

> **en appel**
> appellate level (at)

appelant
appellant
In an appeal case the name of the appellant comes first followed by that of the respondent.

apporter des preuves
adduce evidence (to)
The plaintiff adduced new evidence.

arbitrage
arbitration
An arbitration between employers and employees.

> **porter en arbitrage**
> to go to / to submit to arbitration

arbitre
arbitrator
An arbitrator is someone chosen to settle a dispute.

argument
case
A part of the defence case was rebutted.

arrestation
arrest
A person is under arrest or is not under arrest, there is no intermediate stage.

> **arrestation illégale**
> illegal arrest
> *A US citizen can sue the administration for illegal arrest.*

> **en état d'arrestation**
> under arrest

arrêter
arrest (to)

> **arrêter des poursuites**
> to stay criminal proceedings
> *They decided to stay criminal proceedings.*

assignation
writ
There are two main categories of writs: writs of summons and judicial writs.

> **signifier une assignation à qqn**
> to serve a summons on someone
> *Serving a summons on a person means that this person is ordered to appear in court at a specified place and time.*

audience
court hearing
This court hearing should have been televised.

> **registres d'audience**
> court records

autopsie
post-mortem (examination)
A post-mortem (examination) is a medical examination of a dead person's body in order to find out how he / she died.

banc des accusés
dock
The dock is the place where the person accused of a crime stands or sits.

casier judiciaire
criminal record
This man has got a clean criminal record.

casser en appel une peine ou une déclaration de culpabilité
quash (to)
The Criminal Court has powers to quash convictions.

casser un arrêt
quash (to)
The Cour de cassation quashed the ruling of the Paris Court of Appeal.

cause (= motif)
ground
Adultery is a ground for divorce.

cause directe
proximate cause
The proximate cause of the accident was the bad shape of the road.

cause d'une instance
cause of action

champ d'application
scope
That is within the scope of the new law.

charge de la preuve
burden of proof / onus of proof
The burden of proof is the responsibility for convincing the court of the veracity of the fact alleged.

chef d'accusation
count
The count of murder was withdrawn.

citation à comparaître
summons
One way of bringing a person to trial is by the issuing of a summons.

clause
clause
A clause is a section of a legal document.

clause conditionnelle
conditional clause

commencement de preuve
prima facie evidence
Prima facie evidence is also called presumptive evidence.

communication de documents entre les parties en litige
discovery (of documents)
The discovery is the disclosure by a party to civil litigation of the documents in his possession.

comparaître
appear (to)
He appeared as a witness in this case.

compétence (avoir)
have jurisdiction (to) / be empowered (to)
Courts have jurisdiction to try public officers.

> **être en dehors de la compétence de**
> to come / to fall outside a court's jurisdiction

> **hors de la compétence de**
> ultra vires
> *Ultra vires acts are invalid.*

> **relever de la compétence d'un tribunal**
> to come under / to fall within a court's jurisdiction / the court's ambit

compétence en appel
appellate jurisdiction

compétence en matière civile / pénale
civil / criminal jurisdiction

compétence en première instance
original jurisdiction
The Supreme Court has original jurisdiction when an ambassador is involved.

conclusions écrites (exposé des faits du litige et des prétentions des parties)
pleading
A pleading is a formal written statement in a civil action served on each party by his opponents containing the allegations of fact on which the party pleading relies.

confirmer (un jugement)
affirm (to) / confirm (to)
The Court of Appeal affirmed / confirmed the decision of the High Court.

contrevenant (pénal)
offender
An offender is someone who has committed a crime.

décerner un mandat d'arrêt
issue an arrest warrant (to)
In order to arrest someone a warrant must be issued by a magistrate.

décision (d'un tribunal)
ruling
The judge gave his ruling.

> **rendre une décision**
> to give / to hand down a ruling

décret
decree
A decree is a court order.

défaut de comparution (par)
for want of prosecution

défendeur
defendant
A defendant is a person against whom court proceedings are brought.
respondent
The respondent is the defending party in an appeal or petition to the courts.

déférer pour jugement
commit for trial (to)
Committing for trial may take a short form under the Criminal Justice Act 1967.

délit / infraction
offence / crime
An offence / a crime refers to any illegal action.

délit civil
tort
The law of tort is mainly concerned with providing compensation for personal injury and property damage caused by negligence.

délit grave
misdeed
A misdeed is a very serious offence.

délit pénal
offence
Offences may be classified as indictable or summary.

demande d'une déclaration de mise en état
summons for directions
A summons for directions provides an opportunity for the court to consider the preparation for the action for trial.

demandeur au civil
plaintiff
In civil cases the plaintiff seeks compensation for a loss or injury he has suffered.

demandeur au pourvoi
appellant
An appellant is a person who makes an appeal to a court.

déni de justice
miscarriage of justice
A miscarriage of justice is a wrong decision made by a court which has the result that an innocent person is punished.

déposition
testimony
A testimony is a statement of a witness in court.

détention provisoire (maintenir en)
remand in custody (to)
An accused person may be remanded in custody or released on bail while awaiting trial.

dommageable
wrongful
The law may not necessarily punish a person for committing a wrongful act when he evidently did not intend to do so.

droit (fond du)
substantive law
Substantive law is the part of the law that deals with matters that are not matters purely of practice and procedure.

droit procédural
adjective law
Adjective law is the part of the law that deals with procedure in the courts.

empreintes digitales
fingerprints
The burglar was careful leaving no fingerprints.

enquête menée par un Coroner
inquest
An inquest is an inquiry into a death the cause of which is not known.
A judicial inquiry was opened.

enquête de police
investigation
The results of the inspector's investigation are not known yet.

enquête judiciaire
inquiry

exécuter un mandat d'arrêt
carry out a warrant of arrest (to)
The police immediatly carried out the warrant of arrest issued by the judge.

inculpation
charge
A charge is a formal accusation of a crime.

inculpé (nom)
the accused
Will the accused please stand ?

inculper de
charge with (to)
He was charged with attempted murder.

instance (demande introductive d')
statement of claim
In civil procedure, the plaintiff must serve a statement of claim on the defendant within 14 days of serving the writ.

intenter une action en justice
bring proceedings (to) / initiate proceedings (to) / go to court (to)
He brought proceedings against his employer for unfair dismissal.

intention criminelle
mens rea
Mens rea is the state of mind that the prosecution must prove a defendant to have had at the time of committing a crime in order to secure conviction.

interrogatoire principal du témoin
examination-in-chief
In court a witness is subject to examination-in-chief, cross-examination and reexamination.

> **contre-interrogatoire**
> cross-examination

> **nouvel interrogatoire**
> re-examination

interroger
question (to)
The police officer is questioning the suspect.

intimé
respondent
Leave to appeal to the house of lords may be given to either party, the appellant or respondent.

irréfragable
irrebuttable
Irrebuttable evidence.

irréfutable
irrecusable
Irrecusable testimony.

légal
lawful
He did not use lawful means to persuade his employer not to dismiss him.

légalement
lawfully

légitime
legitimate
Legitimate rights.

litige
litigation
Litigation is the taking of legal action by a litigant.

litigieux
debatable
A debatable case.

mandat
warrant
A warrant is an official document which authorizes somebody to do something.

mandat d'arrêt
arrest warrant

mandat de perquisition
search warrant

mineur
infant / minor
An infant / A minor is a child under the age of 18.

mise en liberté sous caution
bail
The conditions governing bail are contained in the Bail Act 1976.

motif
ground
Adultery is a ground for divorce.

> **au motif de**
> on the ground of

nier une allégation de fait
traverse (to)
To traverse is to deny an allegation of fact made in the pleading of the opposite party.

partie
party
The party in court.

partie lésée
aggrieved party

personne morale
artificial person / juristic person
A juristic / artificial person is an entity such as a corporation.

personne physique
natural person
A natural person is a human being.

plaider coupable
plead guilty (to)
The Magistrates' Courts Act 1980 enables the accused to plead guilty in certain cases without attending court.

plaider non coupable
plead not guilty (to)

plaideur
litigant
The State provides litigants with the courts of law in which they may enforce their rights.

plaidoirie
address to the court
The counsel for defence stood up and gave his address to the court.

plaignant
plaintiff
A plaintiff is a person applying for relief against another person in any form of court proceeding.

plainte
complaint
A complaint is made before a Justice of the Peace or before a clerk to the Justice.

> **porter plainte**
> to lodge a complaint

point
issue
Another issue was raised during the trial.

> **le point en litige**
> the point at issue

poursuites civiles / pénales
civil / criminal proceedings

poursuites pénales
prosecution
The Prosecution of Offences Act 1985.

poursuivre (au civil)
sue (to)
A solicitor may sue his client to be given his fees.

poursuivre (au pénal)
prosecute (to)
In Great Britain the Attorney General can prosecute for criminal actions related to offences against the State, public order and corruption.

pourvoi
appeal
Admissible appeal.

prescription
the doctrine of laches
The doctrine of laches is based on the fact that "delay defeats equity".

présomption
presumption
Almost every presumption holds good only in the absence of contrary evidence.

preuve
evidence [U]
Evidence is all the legal means which tend to prove or disprove a fact.
proof
A proof is the means by which the existence or nonexistence of a fact is established.

> **qui se rapporte à la preuve**
> evidential

> **règle de la preuve par ouï-dire**
> hearsay rule

preuve irrecevable
inadmissible evidence

preuve irréfragable
irrebuttable evidence

preuve recevable
admissible evidence

prévenu
accused (the)
The accused refers to the person who is tried in a court for a crime.

procédure
procedure
Procedure is the formal manner in which legal proceedings are conducted.

procès
trial
A trial is the examination by a court of a civil or criminal case.

> **nouveau procès**
> retrial
> *If the appeal is allowed, the court may reverse the decision of the lower court, amend it or order a new trial.*

procès entaché d'un vice de procédure
mistrial

procès-verbal
record
A record is the documents constituting an authentic account of the proceedings before a court.

quitter la barre
stand down (to)
The witness stood down after giving his testimony.

reconnaissance d'une responsabilité
admission of liability

reconnaissance d'un fait
admission

reconnaître un fait (civil)
admit (to)
Within 14 days of service of the statement of claim, the defendant must serve a defence on the plaintiff. He may admit, traverse, confess and avoid or object in point of law each allegation.

reconstituer
reconstruct (to)
The investigation magistrate reconstructed the events leading to the murder.

recours juridique
legal redress / remedy / relief
Any of the methods available at law for the enforcement, protection or recovery of rights is called remedy / redress / relief.

> **recours porté devant**
> appeal lying to
> *Appeal lying to the Crown Court.*

> **sans aucun recours**
> remediless

recouvrement
recovery
Recovery of premises.

récusation
challenging

récuser
challenge (to)
The prosecution and the defence may challenge prospective jurors.

règle de fond
substantive rule
cf. « fond du droit »

règle de forme
adjective rule
cf. « droit procédural »

règlement à l'amiable
friendly / out of court / amicable settlement

régler des différends
accomodate (to) / settle disputes (to)
The function of a judge is to accomodate / to settle disputes which arise between two parties.

rejeter un appel
dismiss appeal (to)
The Criminal Division has powers to dismiss appeals.

renvoi
referral
The referral by the court of the case to another court.

renvoi
cf. « ajournement »

réparation
redress / remedy / relief
A civil remedy / redress / relief may be granted by a court to a party to a civil action.

> **demander réparation de**
> to seek redress for

requérir
claim (to)

requête
claim
A claim is a demand for a remedy or assertion of a right.

> **partie requérante**
> claimant

réquisitoire
case for the prosecution

ressort (en dernier)
without appeal
Supreme courts decide without appeal.

restitution
cf. « recouvrement »

résumé d'une affaire pénale fait par le juge aux jurés avant la délibération de ceux-ci
summing-up
The summing-up is the last speech which the jurors hear before they retire to consider their verdict.

saisir une juridiction
refer a case to a court (to)
Under the EEC Treaty, a court may refer to the Court of Justice of the European Community a question of community law for a preliminary ruling.

serment
oath
The usual witness's oath is: "I swear by Almighty God that the evidence which I shall give shall be the truth, the whole truth and nothing but the truth."

> **affirmer sous serment**
> to swear on oath

> **faire prêter serment à qqn**
> to put someone on oath

> **prêter serment**
> to take an oath

> **sous serment**
> on / under oath

suspect (adj.)
suspicious
Suspicious circumstances.

suspect (nom)
suspect
They have a suspect for the murder.

suspendre
adjourn (to)
A hearing may be adjourned to a fixed date or sine die.

suspension
stay of proceedings
A stay of proceedings is an order by the court suspending proceedings, usually because of some misconduct by the plaintiff.

témoin
witness
A reliable witness.

> **être témoin**
> to witness

> **suborner un témoin**
> to bribe / to suborn / to tamper with a witness

> **venir à la barre des témoins**
> to take the witness stand

témoin à charge
witness for the prosecution

témoin de fait
material witness

témoin oculaire
eye witness

témoignage
testimony / testimonial evidence
A testimony / testimonial evidence is a statement of a witness in court offered as evidence of the truth of what is stated.

> **faux témoignage**
> false evidence

témoigner de
bear witness (to) / give evidence (to)

2

INFRACTIONS ET DÉLITS CIVILS
OFFENCE AND CIVIL WRONGS

abus de confiance
breach of trust
A breach of trust need not be deliberate or dishonest.

abusif
wrongful
Wrongful dismissal.

> **poursuite abusive**
> malicious prosecution
> *A person who has been convicted of a criminal charge cannot sue for malicious prosecution.*

acte délictueux
tortious act
A tortious act has the nature of a tort.

actes de violence caractérisés
aggravated assault
Aggravated assaults carry stricter penalties than ordinary assaults.

adultère
adultery
Adultery may be evidence of breakdown of marriage.

arme
firearm
The Firearms Act 1968.

assassinat
murder / assassination / murder with malice aforethought
There is a rising number of murders in the USA.

> **tentative d'assassinat**
> attempted murder

atteinte au droit
wrong
Legal wrongs may be criminal or civil.

> **sans acte contraire au droit**
> without legal wrong

atteinte au droit public
public nuisance
Public nuisance is a crime.

atteinte directe
trespass
Trespass is a wrongful direct interference with another person or with his possession of land or goods.

attentat à la pudeur
indecent assault
If committed against a woman, indecent assault is punishable by up to two years' imprisonment.

attenter à la pudeur
assault indecently (to)

auteur d'une infraction
offender
An offender is someone who has committed a crime.

avortement
abortion
In the US pro-lifers are against abortion.

bon père de famille
reasonable man
A reasonable man is an average responsible citizen.

cambriolage
burglary
Burglary is entering a building as a trespasser with intent to steal therein.

chantage
blackmail
Blackmail is punishable by up to one year's imprisonment.

chapardage
pilfering
This young woman is keen on pilfering from supermarkets.

complice de (être)
aid and abet (to)
To aid and abet is to assist in the performance of a crime either before or during its commission.

complot
conspiracy

comploter
conspire (to)
Conspiring is agreeing with another person to commit a crime or tort.

comportement gravement négligent
recklessness
Recklessness means being aware of the risk of a particular consequence arising from one's actions but deciding nonetheless to continue with one's actions and take the risk.

conduite dangereuse
reckless driving

conduite en état d'ivresse
drunken driving
Drunken driving covers two separate legal offences: driving while unfit and driving over the prescribed limit.

conspirer
cf. « comploter »

contravention de simple police
minor offence
A minor offence carries a maximum fine of £1000 or 6 months' imprisonment.

contrebande
smuggling
Smuggling jewels into Switzerland.

contrefaçon
forgery
The Forgery and Counterfeiting Act 1981.

contrefaire
forge (to)

contrevenant
cf. « auteur d'une infraction »

corrompre
bribe (to)

corruption
bribery
Bribery is an offence under the Public Bodies Practices Act 1889.

coups et blessures
assault and battery
The young man was charged with assault and battery.

crime
indictable offence
An indictable offence is an offence that may be tried on indictment i.e. by a jury in the Crown Court.

délictueux (acte)
tortious act
A tortious act has the nature of a tort.

> **agir de manière délictueuse**
> to act in a tortious manner

délit civil
civil wrong / tort
An example of civil wrong is a breach of contract.

> **auteur d'un délit**
> tortfeasor

> **coauteur d'un délit**
> joint tortfeasor

délit pénal
offence
Offences against the person, against public order, etc.

délit pénal grave pouvant entraîner une arrestation sans mandat
arrestable offence
An arrestable offence is one which carries a sentence of at least 5 years' imprisonment.

délit pénal mineur
non-indictable offence

détérioration volontaire
wilful damage

détournement d'avion
hijacking
The Hijacking Act 1971.

détournement de biens
conversion of goods
Conversion of goods is wrongfully dealing with a person's goods.

détournement de fonds
embezzlement
Embezzlement is now classified as a form of theft.

diffamation
defamation
Defamation is usually in words but pictures or gestures can also be defamatory.

diffamation écrite
libel

diffamation verbale
slander

diffamatoire
defamatory

> **propos diffamatoires**
> defamatory statement

diffamer
defame (to) / slander

discrimination
discrimination
Discrimination consists in treating one or more members of a specified group unfairly as compared with other people.

dommage
damage
Damage means loss or harm.

> **causer un dommage**
> to cause damage /
> to make injury / to do mischief

> **évaluer le dommage**
> to assess the damage

> **réparer un dommage**
> to make good a damage

> **subir un dommage**
> to be harmed

dommage aux biens
damage to property

dommage corporel
personal injury

dommage matériel
material damage

dommage réel
actual damage

dommage subi
suffered / sustained damage

dommageable
injurious / wrongful

émeute
riot
Riot is a form of breach of the peace.

enlèvement
abduction
Abduction is taking an unmarried girl under 16 from the possession of her parents or guardian against her will.

entente délictueuse
cf. « complot »

erreur
mistake
A mistake is a misunderstanding or erroneous belief about something.

> **induire délibérément en erreur**
> to give a false impression

erreur de bonne foi
genuine mistake

erreur de droit
mistake of law
In criminal cases, if a person makes a mistake of law and commits a crime because he does not know that it is forbidden by law, he is usually found guilty.

erreur de fait
mistake of fact
A mistake of fact is a misunderstanding about a matter of fact.

évasion
escape
Escape is the offence of escaping from lawful custody.

falsifier
cf. « contrefaire »

faute de la victime
contributory negligence
The effect of contributory negligence is to reduce the plaintiff's damages to an amount that the court thinks just and equitable.

faux et usage de faux (poursuivre pour)
prosecute for forgery (to)
He was prosecuted for forgery and was sentenced to 10 years' imprisonment.

faux témoignage
perjury
Perjury is the offence of giving false evidence.

harcèlement sexuel
sexual harassment
In France, according to a recent survey, sexual harassment is a plague for 22% of working women.

homicide
homicide
A British citizen may be tried for homicide anywhere in the world.

homicide involontaire
excusable homicide / manslaughter
Excusable homicide / manslaughter is the killing of a human being that results in no criminal liability.

illégal
unlawful
An unlawful arrest.

illicite
wrongful
Wrongful possession.

impliqué (être)
be involved (to)
An ambassador was involved in the case.

incendie criminel
arson
Arson carries a maximum sentence of life imprisonment.

incitation à la haine raciale
incitement to racial hatred
Incitement to racial hatred is a crime punishable with up to 2 years' imprisonment.

infraction pénale
cf. « délit »

infraction jugée devant la Magistrates' Court
summary offence
Summary offences are tried without a jury.

insinuation malveillante
innuendo
Innuendoes pervaded the candidate's campaign.

intention
intention
The law will, in certain cases, punish as criminal acts the intention to perpetrate a crime.

> **avec intention de nuire**
> with malice

ivresse
intoxication
Intoxication is not a defence if a person drinks or takes drugs in order to give himself courage to commit a crime.

> **en état d'ivresse publique**
> drunk and disorderly

manquement
breach
A breach is a failure to perform one's obligations.

manquement à l'obligation de prudence
negligence
Negligence is failure to do something that a reasonable man would do, or doing something that a reasonable man would not do.

menaces de voies de fait
assault
Assault is a form of tresspass to the person.

meurtre
murder
Murder is unlawful killing of a person where there is intent to kill.

obligation de vigilance
duty of care
Doctors have a duty of care to their patients.

occupation de fait de la maison d'autrui
squatting
A couple of homeless people were squatting an empty house.

> **personne qui occupe la maison d'autrui**
> squatter

outrage à magistrat
contempt of court
The Contempt of Court Act 1981.

outrage aux bonnes mœurs
outraging public decency
Mounting an indecent exhibition is outraging public decency.

outrage aux mœurs
indecency
Indecency might include staging an indecent exhibition or indecent exposure.

parjure
perjury
The Perjury Act 1911.

piratage
piracy
Piracy may be committed against a ship, or an aircraft; it is also the infringement of copyrights.

pratiques immorales
corrupt practices
Corrupt practices include bribery and intimidation.

préjudice
cf. « dommage »

préjudiciable à qqn (être)
harm somebody (to)

préméditation
malice aforethought
Malice aforethought is the state of mind required for a person to be guilty of murder.

prise d'otages
taking of hostages
The taking of hostages is an extraditable offence.

pornographique
obscene
Under the Obscene Publications Acts 1959 and 1964, it is an offence to publish obscene books.

propos injurieux
abusive words
Abusive words are rude or unkind.

prostitution
prostitution
Prostitution itself is not a crime but soliciting or loitering are.

rapt
kidnapping
Kidnapping is a common-law offence punishable with a maximum sentence of life imprisonment.

relation de causalité
remoteness of damage
The extent to which a defendant is liable for the consequences of his wrongful act is called remoteness of damage.

responsabilité
liability
Examples of liability are: business liability, parents' liability, etc.

> **la responsabilité est retenue contre...**
> the defendant is liable...

responsabilité civile
tortious liability

responsabilité conjointe
joint liability

responsabilité conjointe et solidaire
joint and several liability

responsabilité du fait d'autrui
vicarious liability

responsabilité objective
strict liability

responsabilité séparée
several liability

responsable
liable

rixe
affray
Affray covers such acts as fights between rival football supporters.

rupture
cf . « manquement »

séquestration
false imprisonment
False imprisonment includes unlawful arrest.

sodomie
sodomy / buggery
It is an offence to assault anyone with the intention of committing buggery / sodomy.

subornation de témoins
subornation of perjury
Subornation of perjury is a special statutory offence.

tentative
attempt
Attempt is an offence even if the attempted offence has not been committed.

tentative d'évasion
attempt at escape

tentative de viol
attempted rape

terrorisme
terrorism
The Suppression of Terrorism Act 1978.

trafic de drogue
drug trafficking
They suspect him of drug trafficking.

> **faire un trafic**
> to peddle
> *A person who peddles drugs sells illegal drugs.*

trahison
treason
The penalty for treason is death, but the monarch may exercise the prerogative of mercy.

tromperie
deception
Deception is a false representation, by words or behaviour, of a matter of fact or law that is deliberate or reckless.

viol
rape
A 14-year-old rape victim.

vol
theft
Theft is dishonestly appropriating property belonging to another person with the intention of permanently depriving the other person of it.

vol à l'étalage
shoplifting
Shoplifting is dishonestly removing goods from a shop without paying for them.

vol avec effraction
burglary
They were found guilty of burglary.

vol avec port d'arme
aggravated burglary

vol qualifié
robbery
Robbery is using force against someone in order to commit a theft.

voleur
robber / thief

volontaire
wilful
Wilful damage.

> **involontaire**
> unwilful

3

SENTENCES, VERDICTS ET PEINES
JUDGMENTS, VERDICTS AND SENTENCES

acquittement
acquittal
Acquittal is a decision by a court that a defendant accused of a crime is innocent.

acquitter
acquit (to)

administrateur judiciaire
receiver
The appointment of a receiver enables a judgment creditor to obtain payment of the amount due to him.

amende
fine
A fine is a sum of money that an offender is ordered to pay on conviction.

amnistie
amnesty
Amnesty is frequently granted to groups of people in respect of political offences.

circonstances atténuantes
mitigating circumstances
The judge has accepted mitigating circumstances for this first offender.

complicité
aiding and abetting
It is not necessary to have a criminal motive to be guilty of aiding and abetting.

conclusions
findings
The findings of the court were not in his favour.

condamnation (déclaration de culpabilité)
conviction
Previous convictions.

condamnation (peine)
sentence
Sentence must be pronounced in open court by the presiding judge.

condamné pour
convicted of

condamner (déclarer coupable)
convict (to)

condamner à une peine
sentence (to)

confirmer un jugement
affirm (to) / confirm (to)
The Court of Appeal affirmed / confirmed the decision of the High Court.

confiscation
forfeiture
Forfeiture is loss of property or a right as a consequence of an offence or of the breach of an undertaking.

connaissance de cause (en)
knowingly

coupable
guilty
The accused pleaded guilty.

> **avec intention coupable**
> done with a guilty intent

> **non coupable**
> not guilty
> *Not guilty is a verdict finding that an accused person has not committed the offence with which he was charged.*

dédommagement
compensation
Compensation is monetary payment to compensate for loss or damage.

dédommager
compensate (to)

> **débiteur des dommages et intérêts et frais à la suite d'une décision de justice**
> judgment debtor
> *A judgment debtor is a person against whom a court judgment has been entered,ordering him to pay money that he owes.*

délinquant primaire
first offender

dette issue d'un jugement et dont doit s'acquitter la partie condamnée
judgment debt

dispense de peine
absolute discharge
In an absolute discharge, the defendant is completly free of any criminal liability in respect of the offence and may not subsequently be punished for it.

dispense de peine conditionnelle
conditional discharge
A conditional discharge releases the defendant without punishment, on condition that he is not convicted of any other offence within a specified period.

dommages et intérêts
damages
Damages are awarded by a court as compensation for a tort or a breach of contract.

> **accorder des dommages et intérêts**
> to award damages

dommages et intérêts à titre exemplaire
exemplary damages

dommages et intérêts à valeur répressive
punitive damages

dommages et intérêts fixés au préalable
liquidated damages

dommages et intérêts insignifiants
nominal damages

dommages et intérêts non fixés au préalable
unliquidated damages

dommages et intérêts pour préjudice moral
damages for pain and suffering

dommages et intérêts réduits au strict minimum / franc symbolique
contemptuous damages

emprisonnement
imprisonment
Rape is a crime which may attract a term of imprisonment of at least 5 years.

entraîner
carry (to) / attract (to)
This minor offence carries / attracts 6 months' imprisonment.

erreur judiciaire
miscarriage of justice
A miscarriage of justice is a wrong decision taken by a court which punishes an innocent person.

exécution d'un jugement
enforcement of a judgment

> **faire exécuter un jugement**
> to enforce a judgment
> *Judgments for possession of land may be enforced by writ of possession.*

exécutoire
enforceable

grâce
pardon (royal)
Pardon is the withdrawal of a sentence or punishment by the sovereign under the prerogative of mercy.

inculpé (non condamné, présumé encore innocent)
unconvicted

indulgence
leniency

indulgent
lenient
The Criminal Justice Act 1988 introduced appeal by the Crown against a lenient sentence.

jugement
judgment
Mr Justice X gave his judgment yesterday.

> **confirmer un jugement en appel**
> to affirm / to uphold a judgment

> **modifier un jugement en appel**
> to vary a judgment

> **rendre un jugement**
> to deliver / to pass / to give / to pronounce judgment

jugement définitif
final judgment

jugement mis en délibéré
reserved judgment

jurisprudence
caselaw
Caselaw is the body of law set out in judicial decisions as distinct from statute law.

légitime défense
self-defence
"Self-defence is a defence to charges of offences against the person when reasonable force is used to defend oneself."

libération conditionnelle
parole
Since 1967 prisoners have been able to benefit from the system of parole.

> **faire bénéficier d'une libération conditionnelle**
> to release on parole

mettre à l'épreuve
put on probation (to)

mise à l'épreuve
probation
The idea of probation is that it avoids passing prison sentences on minor offences.

mise en demeure de s'acquitter d'une dette
judgment summons
"A judgment summons is a summons, issued on the application of a person entitled to enforce a judgment, that requires a judgment debtor to appear and be examined on oath as to his means."

négligence
negligence
Negligence is failure to do something that a reasonable man would do.

obligatoire
mandatory
Certain offences such as murder, manslaughter, arson, robbery and rape carry mandatory sentences of imprisonment.

ordonnance de mise sous séquestre
writ of sequestration

ordonnance de saisie de biens immobiliers
writ of possession

ordonnance de saisie-exécution
writ of execution
A writ of execution is a writ used in the enforcement of a judgment.

ordonnance de saisie mobilière
writ of fieri facias

peine
sentence
A sentence is the judgment of a court stating the punishment to be imposed on a defendant who has pleaded guilty to a crime or has been found guilty by the jury.
penalty
A penalty is a punishment for a crime.

term
A short prison term.

> **prononcer une peine**
> to pass sentence

peine de mort
death penalty / capital punishment
Capital punishment for murder was abolished in France in 1981.

peine de prison
custodial sentence
Offences carrying custodial sentences.

peine non privative de liberté
non custodial penalty

peine privative de liberté
custodial penalty

prisonnier
prisoner

prisonnier politique
detainee
A detainee is someone who is held prisoner by a government because of his political views or activities.

récidiviste
persistent / habitual offender
A persistent / habitual offender is a person whose previous criminal record makes him liable to be given an extended sentence of imprisonment.

réclusion à perpétuité
life imprisonment
Life imprisonment is punishment of a criminal by imprisonment for the rest of his life.

remise de peine
remission
All prisoners except those serving life sentence are eligible for remission of one third of their sentence.

rendre une ordonnance
make an order (to)
The Justice of the Peace has made an order in a divorce case.

rendre un verdict
bring in (to) / return a verdict (to)
After a three-hour deliberation the jury brought in / returned a verdict of not guilty.

réparation
relief / redress / remedy
A civil remedy / redress / relief may be granted by a court to a party to a civil action.

> **accorder réparation**
> to grant / to give relief

> **réparer un préjudice**
> to grant relief for injury

responsabilité
liability
Liability for a crime.

retirer le permis de conduire
disqualify from driving (to)
In the case of many driving offences, the court has discretion to disqualify drivers for a stated period.

retrait du permis de conduire
disqualification from driving

saisie
seizure
Seizure is the act of taking possession of something according to a judge's order.

saisie de biens
seizure of property

saisir, opérer une saisie
seize (to)

sanction
punishment
The European Convention on Human Rights forbids the use of "inhuman or degrading" punishment.

sursis
suspended sentence

> **prononcer une peine avec sursis**
> to suspend sentence
> *A sentence of imprisonment may be suspended in certain cases, it is reserved for cases where the term of imprisonment is of two years or less.*

sursis à exécution
stay of execution
Stay of execution is an order suspending the execution of the order of a court.

verdict
verdict
Unanimous verdict.

> **annuler un verdict**
> to set aside a verdict

DROIT CONSTITUTIONNEL

CONSTITUTIONAL LAW

1

TERMES D'USAGE COURANT
USUAL TERMS

Administration publique
Civil Service
The Civil Service of a country consists of all the government departments and all the people who work in them.

assemblée
assembly
An assembly of senators.

bicaméral
bi-cameral
Lots of countries have bi-cameral assemblies.

bicamérisme
bi-camerism

biparti
bipartite / two-party

bipartisme
bi-partism / two-party system
It is not literally true to say that Great Britain has a two-party system.

Chambre
Chamber / House
The British Parliament consists of two Chambers or Houses.

Chambre basse
Lower House
A money bill must start in the Lower House.

Chambre haute
Upper House
In Great Britain the Upper House is the House of Lords.

chef
leader
The leader of the Opposition.

chef d'État
head of State

citoyen
citizen
A British citizen.

conservateur
conservative / tory (GB)
The leaders of the Conservative and Labour parties in the House of Commons are either past, present, or potential prime ministers.

constitution
constitution
The British constitution is a continuously changing blend of the ancient and modern.

constitutionnel
constitutional
The continuity of its constitutional tradition is a distinctive feature of British political life.

> **anticonstitutionnel**
> anticonstitutional

Cour suprême
Supreme Court (US)
The decisions of the Supreme Court are final and take precedence over those of all other judicial bodies.

démocrate
democrat
In the US, the Democrats tend to be the American political, liberal "left".

démocratie
democracy
Democracy is a system of government in which people choose leaders or make important decisions by voting.

droit
Law
A government in power must act according to Law.

right
"There are fundamental rights above the State, which the State may not infringe." (M. Zander)

droit écrit (GB)
common law
The common law is characterised by a number of maxims, e.g. "ignorance of the law is no defence".

droit non écrit (GB)
statute law
Statute law is law made by Parliament and prevails over common law.

État
State
The Welfare State.

État de droit
Rule of Law
The Rule of Law is the principle that the process of government is bound up with the law and that the law is supreme.

étendue (portée, champ d'application)
ambit
No one has ever considered the ambit of such an Act.

exécutif
executive
The executive branch of the government.

faction
faction
Rival factions.

fédéral
federal
Americans are living under the federal, the State and the local city or county rules.

fédéralisme
federalism

force obligatoire (qui a)
binding
Rules of binding usages.

gouvernement
government
The Thatcher government came to power in 1979.

gouverner
govern (to) / rule (to)
"The Queen reigns but does not rule." Nowadays the power to govern rests squarely with ministers, whose advice the Queen must normally accept.

haut fonctionnaire
senior civil servant
The Cabinet office is composed of four Permanent Secretaries of the Cabinet but also of sixty senior civil servants.

interventionnisme
state-control
State-control as opposed to laissez-faire.

inviolable
inviolable
Inviolable rights as stated in the Bill of Rights.

législatif
legislative
Legislative reforms.

législatif
cf. « pouvoir »

libéral
liberal
The liberal party.

Libéralisme
laissez-faire
Laissez-faire is the policy which is based on the idea that governments should not interfere with business or finance.

Opposition (l')
Opposition (the) / the Shadow Cabinet (GB)
Her Majesty's Opposition.

Parlement
Parliament
In Great Britain the Upper House of Parliament is the House of Lords.

parlementaire (adj.)
parliamentary
A parliamentary session.

parlementaire (nom)
parliamentarian
A Prime Minister generally chooses his Cabinet members from experienced parliamentarians.

parti
party
The Labour party.

plénipotentiaire
plenipotentiary
A plenipotentiary is someone who has full power and authority to act as a representative of a country.

politique (la)
politics
Lots of people have never had the slightest interest in politics.

politique (une)
a policy
The US foreign policy.

porte-parole
spokesman
An EEC spokesman.

pouvoir
power
The Thatcher government came to power in 1979.

> **être au pouvoir**
> to be in office
> *Mrs Thatcher was in office from 1979 to 1990.*

pouvoirs conférés à
powers entrusted in / vested in
The powers vested in him by the State of Florida.

pouvoirs énumérés
enumerated powers
Enumerated powers are those which are specifically defined, stated.

pouvoirs exclusifs
exclusive powers

pouvoirs implicites
implied powers

pouvoir exécutif (le)
Executive (the)

pouvoir judiciaire (le)
Judiciary (the)

pouvoir législatif (le)
Legislature (the)

processus législatif
legislative proceedings
The first step of the legislative proceedings is the bill.

rapport
report
The report of the Royal Commission on the Press.

ratification
ratification
The ratification of a treaty.

ratifier
ratify (to)
This country ratified an agreement to ban the use of chemical weapons.

réforme
reform
This MP called for the reform of the divorce laws.

réformer
reform (to)
Magna Carta was a code of reforming laws.

républicain
republican
In the US, the Republicans form the conservative right wing.

soutien
support
The Democrat party generally draws support from minorities while the Republican party draws it from business interests.

souverain (adj.)
sovereign
He was given sovereign powers.

souverain (nom)
sovereign
A sovereign is the royal ruler of a country.

…té

…overeignty.

traité
treaty
The Maastricht treaty.

transgresser
infringe (to)
The law would be infringed if the Queen tried to rule without Parliament.

travailliste
Labour
The Labour Party has just been defeated for the fourth time.

veto
veto
The President of the US has a veto to override a bill passed by Congress.

violation
violation
Violation of the constitution.

> **en violation de**
> in violation of
> *They blockaded the Mediterranean in violation of international agreements.*

2

L'EXÉCUTIF
THE EXECUTIVE

abdication
abdication

abdiquer
abdicate (to)
Edward VIII had to abdicate in 1936 to marry a divorced woman.

accord
assent
The Prime Minister has given his assent.

ancienneté
seniority
The names of the MPs were listed in order of seniority.

appliquer (faire)
implement (to)
The Prime Minister would like to see his health policy implemented in the next Parliament.

approbation
endorsement
The Prime Minister issued his fullest endorsement of the way the trade union dispute was ended.

approuver
endorse (to)
Both governments endorsed the plan.

arbitre
arbitrator
The Prime Minister acts as an arbitrator when the Cabinet ministers disagree with each other.

audience
audience
Each Tuesday the Queen gives an audience to the Prime Minister.

audiences régulières
regular meetings

budget
budget
We should not cut the education budget.

bureau du cabinet
Cabinet Office
The Cabinet Office is composed of four Permanent Secretaries of the Cabinet.

cabinet
Cabinet
"There can be no friendship between the five top men in a Cabinet", said Lloyd George.

cabinet de coalition
coalition Cabinet
The members of a coalition Cabinet come from different political backgrounds.

cabinet fantôme
Shadow Cabinet
This MP is a member of the Shadow Cabinet.

chancelier
Chancellor
In Great Britain the Lord Chancellor is head of the judiciary, he is also a Cabinet minister and Speaker of the House of Lords.

chancelier de l'Échiquier
Chancellor of the Exchequer

chef d'État
Head of State
A money bill can be passed even if the Head of State does not sign it.

collège électoral
Electoral College
The Electoral College meets in Washington for the final stage of the election.

commis de l'État (grands)
top civil servants

commission
committee
There are two main kinds of committees: standing committee and ad hoc committee.

> **membre de commission**
> committee member

> **réunion de commission**
> committee meeting

compte-rendu
minutes
When the Queen gives an audience to her Prime Minister no minutes are taken.

conformément à
accordance with (in)
The Queen must act in accordance with ministerial advice.

conformément à (la loi)
pursuance of (in)
In pursuance of the provisions of this section.

conformer à (se)
conform to (to)
The role of the Supreme Court is to check that legal decisions conform to constitutional law.

conformité
conformity

> **non conformité**
> disconformity
> *In disconformity to the constitution.*

congédier
dismiss (to)
In strict law, the Queen can dismiss her Prime Minister at pleasure.

conseil
advice
The Queen acts on the advice of the Ministers of the Crown.

conseil des ministres
cabinet
"The agenda for the cabinet is short and brisk – the final result of a long process of distillation by the reports of the civil service." A. Sampson

conseiller
Privy Councillor
A Privy Councillor takes an oath of secrecy to the Sovereign.

conseiller d'État
counsellor of State

contrôle
check
In the US, courts act as a check on the executive.

convention nationale
National Convention
In the US, parties hold Primaries in half of the States; Committees meet in the others. They declare support for one of the Party's candidates and select the members of National Convention.

convoquer
summon (to)
The Prime Minister may summon Cabinets whenever and wherever he pleases.

Couronne (la)
Crown (the)
In Great Britain, the Crown in Parliament is sovereign.

crise
crisis (pl. crises)
An unforeseen crisis.

décès (du souverain)
demise / death
At the demise / death of the Queen, Prince Charles will ascend to the throne.

démission
resignation
A letter of resignation.

démissionner
resign (to)
Lloyd George once threatened to resign.

dépêche
dispatch
A Foreign Office dispatch.

dépenses
expenditure
Public expenditure.

désigner
nominate (to)
The President nominated the new Prime Minister.

dévolu
vested in
Powers vested in the monarch.

différend
conflict
The Cabinet arbitrates conflicts that may exist between secretaries.

discours
speech
The Prime Minister made a speech on the importance of education.

> **faire un discours**
> make (to) / deliver a speech (to)
> *When the President of the US is inaugurated, he delivers his inaugural speech.*

dissoudre
dissolve (to)
The Prime Minister appoints, summons, guides and can eventually dissolve the Cabinet.

dûment
duly
"The provisions of this section have been duly complied with."

exerçable
exercisable
The Queen's power of dismissing her Prime Minister is exercisable only in extraordinary circumstances.

former un gouvernement
form a Cabinet (to) / make a Cabinet (to)
Cabinet-making / Forming a Cabinet is probably the most important part of a Prime Minister's job.

gouverner
rule (to)
The Queen reigns but does not rule.

gouverneur
governor
In the US, a governor is responsible for the political administration of a state.

héritier
heir
The Prince of Wales is heir to the throne.

héritier présomptif
heir apparent to the throne

investir dans ses fonctions
inaugurated (to be) / sworn in (to be)
The President of the US is inaugurated / sworn in on the steps of the Capitol.

invitation de (à l')
at the behest of
"If a Ministry failed to resign or to dissolve at the behest of a hostile House of Commons, it could not for long carry on in Parliament without breaking the law." S. B. Chrimes.

ministère (autre que Department of State)
ministry
The Ministry of Energy.

ministère (important)
Department of State
The Department of Health and Social Security.

ministère de l'Intérieur
Home Office

ministère des Affaires étrangères
Foreign Office

ministériel
ministerial
Ministerial responsibility.

ministre (autre que Secretary)
Minister
Lord Carrington, the Foreign Secretary, together with his junior Ministers, resigned in 1982.

ministre (d'un Department of State)
Secretary of State
The Secretary of State for Defence.

ministre (US)
Secretary / Head of Department

ministre de la Défense
Secretary of State for Defence

ministre de la Justice
Lord Chancellor

ministre de l'Emploi
Secretary of State for Employment

ministre de l'Environnement
Secretary of State for Environment

ministre de l'Industrie et du Commerce
Secretary of State for Trade and Industry

ministre de l'Intérieur
Home Secretary

ministre des Affaires étrangères
Foreign Secretary

ministre des Affaires sociales
Secretary of State for Social Services

ministre des Finances
Chancellor of the Exchequer

ministre sans portefeuille
minister without portfolio
The Lord President of the Council is a minister without portfolio.

ministre siégeant au cabinet
Cabinet Minister

nomination
appointment
By appointment of Her Majesty the Queen.

nommer
to appoint
The Queen appoints her Prime Minister.

ordre du jour
agenda
Each Tuesday, the Queen gives an audience to the Prime Minister. The private secretaries set an agenda but the two need not stick to it.

portefeuille (avoir un)
office (to be in) / hold office (to)
This Secretary of State held office for only one year.

pouvoir (arriver au)
take office (to)
Edith Cresson took office as Prime Minister in 1991.

Premier ministre
rime Minister
Prime Minister Tony Blair.

présidence
presidency
Under Reagan's presidency.

président
president
The president of the US is elected for four years and can be re-elected only once.

présidentiel
presidential
The last presidential election.

prérogative
prerogative
Life peers were created by royal prerogative.

promulgation royale
Royal Assent
When agreement is reached between the Lords and the Commons, the Bill is ready to receive the Royal Assent and become an Act of Parliament.

remaniement ministériel
Cabinet reshuffle
"Cabinet reshuffles are apt to be acclaimed by the press either for their cunning or their aptness." A. Sampson

responsabilité
responsibility
"The underlying principle of the cabinet (...) is that of collective authority or collective responsibility." A. Sampson

responsabilité collective
collective responsibility

responsable
responsible

révoquer
dismiss (to) / remove (to)
The Prime Minister made an attempt to remove / to dismiss her from the Cabinet.

secrétaire du cabinet
Secretary of the Cabinet
The Secretary of the Cabinet is often called "Vice Prime Minister" or "Deputy Prime Minister".

secrétaire permanent du cabinet
Permanent Secretary of the Cabinet
There are four Permanent Secretaries of the Cabinet.

sous-secrétaire
undersecretary
The Prime Minister chooses members of his party to hold office as Cabinet ministers, ministers of State, under secretaries and parliamentary secretaries.

vice président
Vice President
The President of the US is assisted by a Vice President also called the "Veep".

3

LE POUVOIR LÉGISLATIF
THE LEGISLATURE

absence de majorité nette au Parlement
hung Parliament

banc des ministres
front-bench
He was appointed front-bench spokesman on education.

> **ministre siégeant à ce banc**
> front-bencher

banc des députés non ministres
back-bench
The bill did not get support of several Labour back-bench MPs.

> **député siégeant à ce banc**
> back-bencher

Chambre des représentants
House of Representatives
Members of the House of Representatives are elected every two years.

chef de file (député chargé d'assurer la discipline à l'intérieur d'un groupe parlementaire)
Whip
A Whip's primary function is to act as an intermediary between the party leader and his followers.

chef de la majorité ministérielle à la Chambre
Leader of the House (the)
The Leader of the House is generally a Cabinet Minister.

Congrès
Congress
Congress cannot force the President to act and the latter cannot stop a law.

Congrès (membre du)
congressman / congresswoman

convocation au Parlement (envoyée par le Whip)
whip
Whips can be used to summon members to party meetings of all kinds.

convocation impérative
three-line whip

convoquer le Parlement
summon Parliament (to)
A Parliament's life always ends by its dissolution by the sovereign in a proclamation that also summons its successor.

débat
debate
A House of Commons debate.

député
Member of Parliament / MP
In 2007 there were 126 female MPs in the House of Commons.

député en exercice
sitting member

député suppléant
deputy MP

direction de (sous la)
under the leadership of

héréditaire
hereditary
A hereditary peer.

jour de séance (des députés)
sitting day
When Parliament is in session there are five sitting days a week.

législature
life of a Parliament
The life of a Parliament is five years at most.

lord membre d'un comité d'appel de la Chambre des lords
Lord of Appeal in Ordinary / Law Lord
The Law Lords are also called the Lords of Appeal in Ordinary.

lord spirituel
Lord Spiritual
The Archbishop of Canterbury is a Lord Spiritual.

lord temporel
Lord Temporal

manifeste
manifesto
The Party's manifesto.

médiateur
Parliamentary Commissioner for Administration / PCA / Ombudsman
The PCA came into being on April 1st 1967.

membre de la Chambre des représentants
Representative
A Representative is a member of the lower house of Congress.

mettre en accusation en vue d'une destitution
impeach (to)
The Congress can impeach the President by a 2/3 majority.

mettre en minorité
defeat (to)
The Conservative party was defeated again in the General Election of 2005.

mise en accusation en vue d'une destitution
impeachment

motion
motion
A motion is a proposal initiated by MPs.

motion de censure
vote of no confidence

Opposition (l')
Opposition (the)
Opposition Whips.

pair
peer

pairesse
peeress
Life peeresses got into the House of Lords before the other category of peeress.

pairie
peerage
The creation of hereditary peerage is one of the Queen's prerogatives.

passer outre
override (to)
Presidential veto can be overridden by a 2/3 majority in both houses.

président de la Chambre des communes / de la Chambre des représentants
Speaker of the House (the)
The Speaker of the House of Commons is given the exclusive right to decide what a Money Bill is.

question parlementaire
parliamentary question
Parliamentary questions can be written, non-written, supplementary or "Private Notice" questions.

renoncer à
renounce (to) / disclaim (to) / waive (to)
The Peerage Act makes it permissable for a hereditary peer to renounce / disclaim / waive his peerage.

séance consacrée aux questions des parlementaires à l'intention du gouvernement
Parliamentary question time

Sénat
Senate
The American Senate is renewed by thirds every two years.

sénateur
senator
In order to be a senator, you must be over 30, have been a citizen of the USA for at least nine years and must live in the State you represent.

session parlementaire
parliamentary session
The life of a Parliament is divided into sessions, normally of one year each.

> **en session**
> in session

soutenir
support (to)
A Prime Minister is always eager to maintain solid back-bench support.

soutien
support

soutien d'un parti
party backing

subvention parlementaire
parliamentary grant
"If, for example, a Ministry failed to resign or to dissolve at the behest of the House of Commons (...), it could not lawfully obtain sufficient funds without parliamentary grant." S. B. Chrimes

vacances parlementaires
parliamentary vacations

> **partir en vacances parlementaires**
> to go into recess
> *The committee will go into recess for a few weeks.*

vote de confiance
vote of confidence
The government cannot survive without a vote of confidence.

4

LE VOTE DES LOIS
LEGISLATIVE PROCEDURE

abrogation
repeal
The Law Commission can propose the repeal of obsolete enactments.

abroger une loi
repeal a law (to)

adopter (faire)
bring in (to)
The Prime Minister intended to bring in new legislation to control immigration.

adopter un texte de loi
pass an enactment (to)
The enactment was passed by Parliament last spring.

allier à (s')
ally oneself with (to)
When the Labour Party allied itself with the Liberal Party in March 1977, this was called the "Lib-Lab pact".

amendement
amendment
The US Constitution is made of the main body and amendments, ten of which were created at the time when the Constitution itself was written.

amender
amend (to)

article d'une loi
section
In pursuance of the provisions of this section.

assentiment royal
Royal Assent
Bills which have passed through both Houses receive Royal Assent.

chef de la majorité ministérielle à la Chambre
Leader of the House (the)
The Leader of the House is normally a Cabinet Minister.

convocation
whip
The whips are printed instructions that can also be used to summon members to party meetings.

convocation impérative
three-line whip
A three-line whip is a printed instruction wherein a particular vote is trebly underlined as one of major importance.

couloir des « oui »
"Aye" lobby
MPs voting "Aye" go out of the Chamber into the lobby on the right of the Speaker which is called the "Aye" lobby.

couloir des « non »
"No" lobby

débats
proceedings
Most parliamentary proceedings are public in Great Britain.

décret
order
The Parliamentary Elections order, 1991.

déposer un projet de loi
table a bill (to)
This bill was tabled by a Labour MP.

député, chef de file d'un parti, chargé d'assurer la discipline à l'intérieur du groupe parlementaire
Whip
There are Government Whips and Opposition Whips.

discuter un projet de loi
debate a bill (to)
The third reading of the bill was debated yesterday.

disposition
provision
"The provisions of this section have been duly complied with."

écourter les débats
curtail debates (to)
There are three methods of curtailing debates: the ordinary closure, the Guillotine and the Kangaroo.

entrer en application
come into force (to)
Some Acts take effect immediately whereas others include in their text a date when they will come into force.

examiner un projet de loi
give a bill its first (to) / second / third reading
The House gave the bill its second reading today.

exécuter (faire)
enforce (to)
In the mid 60s in the US lots of officials refused to enforce the Civil Rights laws.

exécution
enforcement

exécutoire
enforceable

jurisprudence
caselaw
Caselaw is the body of law set out in judicial decisions.

lecture
reading
The House gave the bill its first reading this morning.

législation
statute law
Statute law is the body of law contained in Acts of Parliament.

loi
enactment / Act of Parliament / law / statute law
A bill passed by Parliament and having received the Royal Assent becomes an Act of Parliament.

loi parlementaire
Act of Parliament
Acts of Parliament are classified by the Queen's Printer as public general Acts, local Acts, and personal Acts.

majorité
majority
In the House of Commons, all questions are decided by a simple majority.

> **> avoir la majorité des voix**
> to carry a division

minorité (être mis en)
be defeated (to)
The motion was defeated by 219 votes to 154.

modifier
modify (to) / alter (to)
This bill will no doubt be modified / altered.

obligatoire (ayant force)
binding
With Magna Carta, the liberties were declared to be permanently binding for ever.

paragraphe
clause
A bill is divided into clauses.

> **> sous-paragraphe**
> sub-clause

passer (faire)
pass (to)
The bill was passed without a division.

procédure / processus législatif
proceedings
The first step of the legislative proceedings is the bill.

projet de loi
bill
There are two sorts of bills: private bills and public bills.

promulgation
enactment
The MPs forced the bill's immediate enactment.

promulguer
enact (to)
The courts administer the laws which Parliament has enacted.

proposer une motion
move a motion (to)
If you move a motion, you formally propose it so that everybody present can vote for or against it.

recueil des lois (votées par le Parlement)
Statute Book
The Statute Book is the entire body of existing statutes.

réexamen d'un projet de loi
report stage
The Report Stage is the moment when the House reconsiders the entire bill.

règle de fond
substantive law
Substantive law is the part of the law that deals with rights, duties and all other matters that are not matters purely of practice and procedure.

règlement
delegated legislation / subordinate legislation
Delegated legislation consists of Orders in Council and instruments of various names (orders, for example).

rejeter
reject (to) / throw out (to)
"A Bill shall.be deemed to be rejected by the House of Lords if it is not passed by the House of Lords". Parliament Act 1911.

résolution
resolution
A resolution is a formal decision taken by means of a vote.

termes de (aux)
under the terms of
Under the terms of the Peerage Act, if there is no male heir to a peerage, then the peerage may go to the eldest daughter.

voix
vote
An equal number of votes.

> **demander la mise aux voix**
> to call for a division

vote (au Parlement)
Division of the House
The Speaker announces that a Division of the House is to take place by giving the order to "clear the lobby".

vote de confiance
vote of confidence

vote de défiance
vote of no confidence

vote prépondérant
casting vote
In the House of Commons if there is an equal number of votes being cast for and against, the Speaker must give the casting vote.

> **sans procéder au vote**
> without a division

voter
vote (to)
In the House of Lords, those voting in favour of a motion are called "Contents".

voter un projet de loi
vote a bill (to)

5

LES ÉLECTIONS
ELECTIONS

abstenir (s')
abstain from voting (to)
In this constituency, 18% of those interviewed decided to abstain from voting.

abstention
abstention

abstentionniste
stay-away voter

bulletin de vote
ballot paper
No mention of party is to be found on the ballot paper.

bureau de vote
polling station
Each elector may cast one vote, normally in person, at a polling station.

campagne
campaign
A political campaign.

candidat
candidate
Meetings still provide the main opportunity for a candidate to make some impressions upon a constituency.

candidat aux élections présidentielles (US)
nominee

circonscription
constituency / ward / district
The UK is divided into constituencies.

collège électoral (US)
Electoral College
The Electoral College meets in Washington for the final stage of the election.

commission chargée du redécoupage électoral
Boundary Commission
There are four permanent Boundary Commissions, one each for England, Scotland, Wales and Northern Ireland.

consignation électorale
deposit
A candidate must give a £500 deposit.

> **perdre sa consignation électorale**
> to lose / to forfeit one's deposit
> *The £500 deposit is lost / forfeited if the votes for the candidate do not exceed 5% of those validly cast.*

convention nationale (US)
National Convention
In the US, committees select the members of National Conventions.

découpage (des circonscriptions)
drawing / districting (US)
Boundary commissions carry out periodic reviews of the drawing of parliamentary constituencies for the purpose of recommending boundary changes to take account of shifts in population.

> **redécouper**
> to redraw / to redistrict (US)
> *The boundaries of a constituency is redrawn every 15 years.*

découpage des circonscriptions pour servir les intérêts d'un parti
gerrymandering
Gerrymandering is the act of altering political boundaries of constituencies in order to give an unfair advantage to one political party.

démissionner
resign (to) / bow out (to) / step down (to)
When a MP resigns / bows out / steps down a by-election takes place.

dépouillement du scrutin
counting of the votes
The counting of the votes used to be carried out manually by the returning officer and his assistants.

> **durant le dépouillement**
> during the count

dissolution
dissolution

dissoudre
dissolve (to) / disband (to)
General elections are held after a Parliament has been dissolved.

> **obtenir la dissolution du Parlement**
> to procure a dissolution of Parliament

droit de suffrage / de vote
franchise
The Representation of the People Act 1985 extends the franchise to British citizens abroad for a period of 5 years after leaving the UK.

> **avoir le droit de vote**
> to be entitled to vote
> *Members of the House of Lords are not entitled to vote for MPs.*

> **perte du droit de vote**
> disfranchise

électeur
elector / constituent
Electors who are physically incapacitated are entitled to vote by post.
A MP is the servant of his constituents.

électeurs (grand) (US)
Presidential Electors
After Election Day, each State will nominate a number of Presidential Electors.

élection
election
He may vote for the female candidate at the next election.

élections législatives (GB)
General Election
General Elections are held after a Parliament has been dissolved.

élection législative partielle
by-election
A by-election is an election that is held to choose a new MP when a member has died or resigned.

électorat
electorate
With proportional representation, MPs would be more representative of the electorate as a whole.

éligibilité
eligibility

éligible
eligible
In order to be eligible for the Senate, you must be over 30, have been a citizen of the US for at least 9 years and must live in the State you represent.

élire
return (to)
Each constituency returns one member to the House of Commons.

> **ré-élire**
> to re-elect

> **ne pas élire**
> to vote out
> *He was voted out by a large majority.*

fraude (électorale)
fraud / ballot-box stuffing (fam.)
Ballot papers are numbered, so that allegations of fraud / ballot-box stuffing may be checked if necessary.

liste électorale
annual register of electors / ticket (US)
A British citizen may not vote if he is not registered in the annual register of electors.

majorité
majority
He was beaten by a large majority.

majorité absolue
overall majority

majorité simple
simple majority
In Great Britain the simple majority system is also called the "first past the post system".

mandat (électoral)
mandate
A powerful Labour mandate.

obligatoire
compulsory
Voting is not compulsory in Great Britain.

obtenir des voix
polls (to)
The candidate who polls the most votes in a constituency is elected.

porte-à-porte
canvassing
The purpose of canvassing is to introduce the candidate.

présenter sur une liste (se)
run on a ticket (to) (US)
He is running on the Democratic ticket.

primaire
primary
In the US, parties hold primaries in half of the States.

procuration (par)
by proxy
Service voters resident abroad and merchant seamen may vote by proxy.

programme électoral
platform
The party's platform.

représentation proportionnelle
proportional representation / PR
Both Conservative and Labour parties are against proportional representation / PR.

scrutateur
counting agent

scrutin
ballot
In Great Britain, elections of MPs are by secret ballot.

> **premier tour de scrutin**
> first ballot

scrutin majoritaire
majority vote system

scrutin uninominal à un tour
single ballot / simple plurality system / simple majority system
The simple majority system is also called the "first past the post system".

siège
seat
At the 2005 elections, Labour got 356 seats whereas Conservative got 198.

ticket (US)
He will be elected on an environmental ticket.

urne
ballot box
A ballot box is a box into which ballot papers are put after people have voted.

DROIT DES CONTRATS

CONTRACT LAW

abus de confiance
breach of trust
A breach of trust is any improper act or omission contrary to the trustee's duty.

accepter
consent (to)
The parties who have consented to the contract are...

accord
agreement
The agreement must be final and certain.

accord irrévocable
binding agreement

accord mutuel (par)
if both parties agree

acte authentique
deed
A deed is a written document that is signed, sealed and delivered.

agir pour
act for (to) / act as the agent of (to)
In a contract, the agent is acting for his principal.

annexe
appendix
A list of suppliers is given in the appendix.

annulable
voidable
Voidable for fraud.

annulation
cancellation / annulment

annulation pour vice du consentement
rescission

annuler un contrat pour vice du consentement
rescind a contract (to)

application de (en)
pursuant to
Pursuant to article 3 of the agreement...

appréciation discrétionnaire
discretion
The agent may refrain from exercising any right, power or discretion...

attendu que
whereas
Whereas Supplier designs and manufactures in Spain...

autoriser
authorize (to) / authorise (to)
The lender authorizes / authorises the agent to exercise such rights...

> **non autorisé**
> unauthorized

avenant
amendment
An amendment is an alteration of a document to correct some error in the original.

cadre (dans le)
under
Under the purchase agreement.

caducité
lapse of offer
A lapse of offer is the termination of an offer as a result of time, death or nonfulfilment of a condition.

cahier des charges
specifications (GB) / requirements (US)
Specifications / requirements give the details and extent of supply in a contract.

au cas où
in the event of / in case
In the event they authorise the agent...

ci-joint
hereto
The specifications attached hereto.

clause
provision / term
The provisions set out hereunder...

clause de non-responsabilité
exemption clause

commettant
principal
The agent arranges a contract between his principal and a customer.

concerne (en ce qui)
by way of (= as)
The sum was received by way of payment of the outstanding invoice.
in respect of (= for)
You can obtain damages in respect of defective goods.

condition
requirement

> **dans les conditions**
> as provided
> *As provided in this contract.*

> **dans les conditions et selon**
> as provided and in accordance with

conditions de paiement
terms of payment
The terms of payment are essential in a contract.

conférer à
vest in (to)
The agent has a variety of powers vested in him.

confidentiel
confidential
All information is confidential, proprietary of user...

confidentialité
confidentiality

consécutif
consequential
Consequential means happening as a direct result of a particular event or situation.

consentir
consent (to)
For there to be a valid contract at common law, the two contracting parties must both consent to the contents of the contract.

contractant
contracting party
One of the contracting parties was induced to enter into the contract by fraud.

contracter (capacité de)
contractual capacity

contractuel
contractual
The link between agent and principal is partly contractual.

contrat
contract
The contracting parties to the contract.

> **confirmer un contrat**
> to affirm a contract

> **exécuter un contrat**
> to perform / to carry out a contract

> **passer un contrat**
> to enter into a contract
> *The defendant and the co-owner entered into a contract to sell the house to the plaintiff.*

contrat (inexécution d'un)
non-completion of a contract

contrat clé en main
turnkey contract

contrat de bail
lease contract

contrat de consultant
consulting agreement

contrat de distribution
distributor agreement

contrat de licence
licence agreement

contrat de location-vente
hire-purchase contract

contrat de louage d'ouvrage
contract for services

contrat de représentation
agency agreement

contrat de société
deed of partnership

contrat écrit
written contract
The written contract did not conform with the agreement.

contrat formel
specialty contract

contrat synallagmatique
synallagmatic / bilateral contract

contrepartie à l'engagement du contractant
consideration
Consideration is an important element in the formation of a contract in Common Law.

convention
agreement
This agreement made this 30th day of April 1992, by and between...

convenu (il est)
it is understood
It is understood that the prices indicated on the buyer's purchase order do not include any sales (...) payable to federal, state or local authorities.

date d'achèvement
completion date

date d'échéance
date of maturity

date d'entrée en vigueur
effective date / date of coming into force
The effective date / the date of coming into force was February 3rd 1990.

délai
time-extension
In the case of delay, client shall be entitled to appropriate time-extension for completion of the service.

demande de (à la)
at the instance of
At the instance of supplier.

devoir de
duty of
Duty of confidentiality.

disposition
provision
Optional provisions.

> **sauf dispositions contraires**
> unless otherwise provided

disposition légale
statutory possibility

dol
fraudulent misrepresentation
In case of fraudulent misrepresentation, the aggrieved party may repudiate the contract.

dommages et intérêts
damages
The plaintiff was entitled to damages for loss of employment.

> **montant des dommages et intérêts**
> award

double
counterpart
The agreement shall become effective upon receipt by us of a counterpart hereof.

engagement
obligation
So long as you are not in default of your obligations hereunder.

engager par contrat (s')
contracts (to)
They contracted to supply us with oil.

entrée en vigueur
entry into force
Four years after the entry into force of this agreement.

entrer en vigueur
effective (to be)
The agreement shall be effective on the date specified below.

erreur
mistake
A mistake as to the identity of one of the contracting parties.

établir
lay out (to)
The conditions laid out in the paragraph below.

éteindre un contrat
discharge a contract (to)
A contract may be discharged if both parties agree.

exclusif
exclusive
Exclusive rights.

exécuter un contrat
carry out (to) / perform (to) / enforce a contract (to)
Under a void contract, neither party comes under any obligation to perform / to enforce / to carry out the contract.

exécution d'un contrat
performance
Performance of the contract was subject to a long delay.

exécution forcée
specific performance
The order for specific performance was discharged.

> **non-exécution**
> non-completion / non-performance

exécution partielle
part performance

exécution suffisante
substantial performance

exécutoire
enforceable
For a bargain to be enforceable at law there must be valuable consideration.

explicite
express

expressément
expressly
The store was bought expressly for his son.

façon (en aucune)
event (in no)
In no event shall the company be liable for any incidental or consequential damages.

faillir à ses obligations
fail to fulfil one's obligations (to)
The other party had failed to fulfil its obligations.

faute
mistake / negligence
The mistake must be sufficiently important for the contract to be void.

faute grave
gross negligence

fiduciaire
fiduciary
The link between principal and agent is partly contractual and partly fiduciary.

foi de quoi (en)
witness whereof (in)
In witness whereof the said parties...

forclos
time-barred
The arbitration proceedings should have started earlier, therefore the buyer was time-barred.

fraude
fraud
Voidable for fraud.

garantie
warranty
Exclusion of warranty.

garantir
warrant (to)
The agent warrants that he has authority...

indemniser
indemnify (to)
The employee was indemnified for his wrongful dismissal.

inexécution d'une obligation contractuelle
default
Default is failure to carry out a contract

interpréter les termes d'un contrat
construe (to)
The terms of the contract can be construed in different ways.

investi
vested
The Agent may refrain from exercising any right, power or discretion vested in it.

jouissance
enjoyment
Quiet enjoyment.

> **avoir la jouissance de**
> to enjoy
> *User shall enjoy the product in accordance with the provisions of this agreement.*

lier
bind (to)
The agreement binds the parties hereto.

mandant
principal
Principal and Agent.

méprise
mistake
A mistake as to the identity of one of the contracting parties.

nommer
appoint (to)
In a contract P (principal) has appointed A (agent) to act for him.

objet (du contrat)
purpose
The purpose of this contract is for the supply of equipment in conformance with the specifications stipulated by customer.

partie
party
One of the parties.

> **les parties du contrat**
> The contractual parties
> *The contractual parties have each named an arbitrator.*

partie lésée
aggrieved party
In case of fraudulent misrepresentation the aggrieved party may repudiate the contract.

perpétuel
perpetual
This licence is perpetual.

personnel
non-transferable
This licence is non-transferable.

place de (à la)
in lieu of
The express warranties contained in this agreement are given in lieu of all other warranties.

postérieur
subsequent to
Subsequent to the date of the contract.

pouvoir
discretion / authority
The Agent warrants that he has authority / discretion to do so.

préavis
notice
Written notice.

préjudice
injury
Irreparable injury.

detriment
The value which takes form of detriment or benefit to the other party.

(par le) présent (acte, document, etc.)
hereby
You hereby purchase from us...

présent contrat (le)
contract (this)
Pursuant to the provisions of this contract.

prévu
provided for
Save for the exceptions or derogations provided for in this contract.

procédure arbitrale
arbitration proceedings
By the contract, the arbitration proceedings should have started earlier.

procuration
power of attorney
A power of attorney is an authority given by one person to another to act on his behalf.

rapidement
promptly
The Agent shall promptly inform the lender of the contents of any document...

reconnaître
acknowledge (to)
You hereby acknowledge that you have made your own credit analysis...

rectifier (un contrat)
rectify (to)
The court had jurisdiction to rectify the contract.

rectification
rectification

rédiger un contrat
draw up (to) / write out (to) / draft a contract (to)
There was a mistake as to the identity of one of the contracting parties when the contract was drawn up / written out / drafted.

renonciation à un droit
waiver
The failure of either party to enforce at any time of the provisions of the Purchase Agreement (...) shall in no way be construed to be a waiver of such provisions...

réserver le droit de (se)
reserve the right to (to)
The company reserves the right to reproduce, publish, sell, license and distribute the product.

résiliation
termination
The termination of the contract was decided by the judge.

résilier
terminate (to)
The contract can be terminated by giving notice.

résolution (d'un contrat)
cancellation / avoidance of a contract

résoluble
annulable
If a contract is annulable, it can be declared invalid.

respecter (les termes d'un contrat)
perform (to) / comply with (to)
Under a void contract, neither party comes under the obligation to perform / comply with it.

responsable
liable
In no event shall the company be liable for any incidental or consequential damages under any circumstances whatsoever.

responsabilité
liability

> **s'exonérer de responsabilité**
> to avoid liability

responsabilité civile
third party risk

responsabilité indivisible
unseverable responsibility

révoquer unilatéralement
repudiate (to)
Repudiating a contract is an anticipatory breach of contract.

rupture (de contrat)
breach
A breach of contract is an actual failure by a party to perform his obligations under that contract or an indication of an intention not to do so.

sceau
seal
Signed, sealed and delivered by the said X.

selon (= conformément à)
accordance with (in) / pursuant to
In accordance with / Pursuant to the provisions of this contract, the supplier shall supply and deliver the goods as described in the specifications attached hereto.

selon (= en vertu de)
under / by virtue of
Under the European Community Act 1972, the UK is bound by rulings of the European Court.

soit ... soit
whether … or
Whether proposed by vendor or purchaser.

sous réserve de
save for
Save for the derogations provided for in this contract.

> **sous réserve de mes droits**
> without prejudice to my rights

soussigné
undersigned
I, the undersigned Mary Taylor, declare...

stipuler
stipulate (to)
The contract stipulates that either party may withdraw at 6 months' notice.

sus-mentionné
aforementioned
The aforementioned conditions.

tacite
implied
Implied acceptance.

termes (d'un contrat)
terms
Subject to the terms and conditions set forth therein.

titre de (au)
under
Under the purchase agreement.

tromperie
fraud
A contract may be voidable for fraud.

valide
valid
This contract is no longer valid.

> **non valide**
> invalid
> *Without stamp duty the document is invalid.*

vertu de (en)
cf. « selon »

vice
defect

> **entaché d'un vice**
> vitiated

vice caché
latent defect
In a sale of goods, the buyer usually has a legal remedy against a professional seller if the goods have a latent defect.

vice de forme
for want of form

vigueur (en)
force (in)

> **entrée en vigueur**
> cf « entrée »

viser (= parapher)
initial (to)
What you have to do is to initial the papers.

DROIT COMMERCIAL
COMMERCIAL LAW

acceptation
acceptance / acquiescence
An acceptance is an agreement to the terms of an offer.

acceptation (refus d')
non-acceptance
A non-acceptance is a wrongful neglect or refusal by the buyer to take possession of the goods by the seller.

acceptation de marchandises
acceptance of goods

acceptation d'offre
acceptance of order

accepteur
acceptor

accessoire, annexe
incidental
Incidental expenses.

accords commerciaux
commercial agreements
Commercial agreements are agreements which are made in a commercial environment.

accord commercial restrictif
restrictive trading agreement
A restrictive trading agreement is subject to registration with the Director General of Fair Trading.

accusé de réception
notice of delivery / acknowledgement of receipt
We have not received the notice of delivery / the acknowledgement of receipt yet.

achat, acquisition
purchase
What is the exact date of purchase?

acheteur
buyer
The buyer is the person in a contract for the sale of goods who has bought or has agreed to buy those goods for a fixed price.

acompte
downpayment
A downpayment is an incomplete payment of a sum which is due to be paid by the buyer to the seller.

acquéreur
buyer
"After receipt of notice by Buyer."

affréteur
charterer
A charterer is a party in a charterparty contract who takes control of somebody else's vessel for the purpose of carrying a cargo.

arbitrage
award
The judgment of an arbitrator is called his award.

arbitre (juge)
referee / arbitrator

armateur
shipowner
The shipowner lets his ship to the charterer for the purpose of carrying a cargo.

assurance
insurance
You'd better ring up your insurance broker.

assurance (police d')
insurance policy

assurance (prime d')
premium
When you apply to an insurance broker you discuss the rate of premium to be paid.

assurance au capital différé
endowment insurance

assurance au tiers
third party insurance

assurance automobile
motor-car insurance

assurance incendie
fire insurance

assurance maritime
marine insurance

assurance obligatoire
compulsory insurance

assurance responsabilité civile
liability insurance

assurance tous risques
comprehensive insurance

assurance vol-incendie
fire and theft insurance

assuré
insured (party)
The insured (party) is surprised at not having received his insurance certificate.

assureur
insurer
If you want to insure your car, you'd better apply to an insurer.

attestation (serment)
affidavit
An affidavit is a sworn written statement.

avenant
rider
The following constitutes a rider to the attached contract and shall be deemed incorporated within.

bailleur de fonds
cf. « commanditaire »

banque
bank
Banks offer different services to their clients.

banque d'affaires
merchant bank

banque de commerce
commercial bank

banque de dépôt
deposit bank

barème
schedule / rate
A schedule is a written list of prices, conditions or details.

bénéficiaire
payee / recipient
The payee is the party to a bill of exchange to whom the money will be paid by the drawee on the directions of the drawer.

bien
property
English law divides property into real property (land for instance) and personal property (goods for instance).

billet à ordre
promissory note
There are two parties to a promissory note.

bonne foi (de)
bona fide
Bona fide is an act done in good faith.

bordereau
slip / note
The slip / note should have been signed.

bordereau (pièce justificative)
voucher

bordereau d'expédition
dispatch note / consignment note

cahier des charges
specifications
Pursuant to Buyer's specifications.

caution
cf. « garantie »

céder
transfer (to)

certificat
warrant
A warrant is a document authorizing the payment of money.

certificat d'entrepôt
warehouse warrant
A warehouse warrant is issued when goods are taken into a public warehouse and must be produced when they are removed.

cessible
transferable
If something is transferable it can be passed to somebody else.

> **non cessible**
> non transferable

cessionnaire
transferee
A transferee is someone who receives a bill of exchange from a person who has either endorsed the bill to the transferee or who has delivered the bill to him.

chambre de commerce
chamber of commerce
The chamber of commerce will give you information on this wholesaler.

charge
encumbrance
A buyer is entitled to take the goods free of any encumbrance.

> **à la charge de**
> borne by
> *"Any expenses incurred in this connection shall be borne by the manufacturer."*

charte-partie
charter party
A charter party is an arrangement by which the owner of a ship either lets his ship to the charterer for the purpose of carrying a cargo or undertakes that his ship shall carry a cargo for the charterer.

chef de file
lead
A lead bank.

clause
clause
We have inserted a clause in the contract that allows us to buy the building back at the original price.

clause de force majeure
force majeure clause

clause pénale
penalty clause

clé en mains
turnkey (GB) / on stream (US)
A turnkey contract.

client
customer
Next spring the customers of this supermarket will find better parking facilities.

commanditaire
sleeping partner
A sleeping partner (in general partnerships) is called limited partner (in limited partnerships).

commandités
active / acting / general partners
Active / Acting / General partners are severally liable to the full extent of their own property.

commerce
trade
Foreign trade.

commission
commission / fee
He gets commission on top of his basic salary.

concessionnaire
distributor / dealer
"The status of distributor is granted to the corporation X..."

concurrence
competition
We have been in competition wih this firm for ages.

concurrence (libre)
free competition

concurrence loyale
fair trading / competition

concurrence déloyale
unfair trading / competition

concurrentiel
competitive

conditions
terms
Terms of payment.

conditions générales et particulières
terms and conditions

conditions habituelles / d'usage
usual terms

conditionnel
conditional
A conditional offer.

conforme
true / up to
True to specimen / up to standard.

connaissement
bill of lading / BL
The bill of lading / BL is an evidence of the contract of affreightment between the shipper and the ship-owner.

contingentement
quota
An import quota of Japanese cars.

contrat
contract
cf. chapitre 4 : Contract law

contrat d'achat
purchase agreement

contrat de vente
agreement for sale

contrefait
forged
A forged endorsement.

contrôle
control
Under government control.

courtier
stock-broker
A stock-broker is a person whose job is to buy and sell stocks and shares for people who want to invest money.

courtier en assurance
insurance broker
For further details on insurance policies, contact your insurance broker.

coût
cost
Beware of the cost of credit!

coût, assurance, frêt / CAF
Cost, Insurance and Freight / CIF
CIF is FOB plus insurance and freight charges to the port of destination.

créance
debt
You should spend less until your debts are paid off.

> **recouvrer une créance**
> to collect a debt

créancier
creditor
This firm was dunned by its creditors.

crédit
credit
A credit sale agreement.

crédit (calendrier d'utilisation du)
paying out scheme

crédit à la consommation
consumer credit

crédit à tempérament
instalment credit

crédit croisé
swap credit

crédit par acceptation renouvelable
revolving credit

date
date
The matter will be discussed at a later date.

date butoir
deadline
This manufacturer never meets the deadline.

date d'échéance
value date

débiteur
debtor
A debtor is a person who has legal liability to pay a sum of money to another person.

découvert (bancaire)
overdraft
An overdraft allows you to spend more money than you have in your bank account.

dédommagement
remedies
"The remedies set forth herein are exclusive."

défaut
default
Default is failure to do something required by law.
defect
In a sale of goods, the buyer generally has a legal remedy against the seller if the goods have a latent defect.

défaut apparent
patent defect

défaut caché
latent defect

défaut de paiement
default of payment

déposant
bailor
A bailor is a person who delivers goods to another under a bailment arrangement.

dépositaire
bailee
A bailee is a person who has possession of goods by virtue of a bailment arrangement.

destinataire
consignee
Could you repeat the consignee's name, please?

détenteur
holder
The stock holder is paid specific interest for a specific length of time.

détériorées (marchandises)
perished goods
Perished goods are goods which have been lost, destroyed or become commercially worthless.

dette
debt
A debt is a sum of money owed by one person for services rendered by another person.

distributeur
distributor
The technicians of the distributor are going to attend training courses.

distribution
distribution
Distribution consists in bringing the goods from the producer to the consumer.

dommages et intérêts
damages
Damages are usually awarded by the courts but can be agreed in advance by parties to a contract.

dommages et intérêts fixés d'avance
liquidated damages

droit de recours
right of recourse / right of legal redress

> **renoncer à tout droit de recours**
> to waive all rights of recourse / redress
> *"Purchaser waives all rights of recourse against supplier."*

droit de vente
right to sell
The right to sell is the unconditional right of the seller to pass the property of the goods to the buyer.

droit de revente
right of resale
The right of resale is the right of an unpaid seller to resell the goods to another person.

échéance
maturity / deadline
Maturity is the time at which a bill of exchange becomes due for payment.

échéance (date d')
date of maturity / due date

effet de commerce
bill of exchange / negotiable instrument
Cheques are examples of bills of exchange / negotiable instruments.

effet de levier
leverage
The leverage effect is the contrary of the boomerang effect.

effets à recevoir
bills receivable
Bills receivable are claims of a firm on its customers.

encaissement (d'effets)
collection / clearing
Handing documents to a bank for collection.

endettement
indebtedness
Purchasing this warehouse is going to involve higher indebtedness than renting.

endos / endossement
endorsement
If you make an endorsement of a document or cheque, you write a note on the document or write your name on the back of the cheque.

endossataire
endorsee

endossé en blanc
blank endorsed

endosser
endorse (to)

endosseur
endorser

engagement
commitment
"If such contingency occurs, the purchaser may (...) buy elsewhere products to be purchased hereunder and deduct from any commitment the quantity purchased elsewhere."

covenant
Covenants may be either express or implied.

entrepôt sous douane
bonded warehouse
Dutiable goods can be stored in a bonded warehouse.

exécution
performance / completion
Once fully carried out, the contract is discharged by performance / completion.

> **non-exécution**
> non-performance / non-completion

> **exécution dans les délais et en bonne et dûe forme**
> proper and timely performance

expédier
dispatch (to) / forward (to) / ship (to)
We'll do our best to dispatch all the units before the end of next week.

expéditeur
consigner

expédition
consignment

expiration
lapse of time
The expiry of a fixed time in which an offer must be accepted is called lapse of time.

fabricant
manufacturer
A farm machine manufacturer.

> **garantie du fabricant**
> manufacturer's guarantee

> **responsabilité du fabricant**
> manufacturer's liability

facture
invoice / bill
Please find enclosed our invoice n° FC48 for $456 for your order n° DL 506.

facturer
invoice (to) / bill (to)

falsifié
forged
A forged endorsement.

faute intentionnelle
wilful misconduct
"Except for fraud or wilful misconduct by Seller neither Seller nor its Supplier will be liable to Purchaser."

fixation collective des prix
price maintenance agreement
A price maintenance agreement is an agreement between a group of people which establishes minimum prices at which goods may be sold or which seeks dealers in these goods to observe the prices.

force majeure
act of God / force majeure
A force majeure clause.

> **cas de force majeure**
> acts of God
> *"Seller shall not be held responsible for any delay or failure in performance hereunder caused by acts of God."*

forfaitaire (commission)
flat fees
Flat advertising fees.

forfaitaire (frais)
lump sum expenses

fortuit
accidental / unplanned / fortuitous / casual
An accidental strike.

fournisseur
supplier
"The supplier shall provide in due time assistance to customer."

> **agrément du fournisseur**
> approval of supplier

frais
charges / costs
Franco to customer's premises covers all transport and handling charges up to the delivery of the goods.

frais de déchargement
unloading charges

frais de gestion
maintenance fees

frais d'entreposage
storage / warehouse costs

frais de manutention
handling charges

frais encourus
expenses incurred
"Any expenses incurred in this connection shall be borne by the manufacturer."

franco bord
free on board / FOB
Free on board / FOB includes transport and loading aboard the ship.

franco quai
free alongside ship

fret
freight
The price includes freight charges.

fusion
merger / amalgamation (US)
A merger / An amalgamation is generally effected by a takeover bid.

fusionner
merge (to)

gage
pledge
A pledge is a loan of money in return for the delivery of possession of goods to the lender of that money.

garant
guarantor
A guarantor is a person who gives a guarantee or who is bound by one.

garantie
guarantee
A guarantee is a contract whereby one person agrees to answer for the debt of another.
warranty
"The terms of warranty execution are as follows..."

security
Security of employment.

> **prolongation de la garantie**
> extension of the warranty

honorer
honour (to)
Their bills have always been honoured.
to meet
He has always met his commitments.

> **ne pas honorer**
> to dishonour
> *When a bill is dishonoured by non-payment, the holder of the bill has a right of recourse against the drawer.*

hypothèque
mortgage
Virtually any property may be mortgaged.

illicite
illicit
They were prosecuted for illicit drug selling.

indemniser
indemnify (to)

> **demande d'indemnisation**
> claim

indemnité
indemnity
An indemnity is a form of compensation given to someone who has incurred losses as a direct result of entering into a contract because of misrepresentation.

indemnité de clientèle
compensation for goodwill
"The distributor shall be entitled to compensation for goodwill equal to x% of the total sales."

insolvabilité
insolvency
When a person has ceased to pay his debts or cannot pay them when they become due, he is in a state of insolvency.

intérêts
interest
Interest rates are much higher in the case of a revolving credit.

intérêts à échoir
accruing interest

intérêt de retard
default interest

intérêts échus
accrued interest

intérêts légaux
statutory interest

intérêts rétroactifs
back interest

lettre de change
bill of exchange
Your bill of exchange falls due at the end of this week.

lettre de crédit
letter of credit

lettre de voiture
waybill
Waybill details will be passed from the cargo computer system through the customs authority computer.

liberté du commerce (atteinte portée à la)
restraint of trade / restrictive trade practices
Restraint of trade limits a person's right to exercise his trade or carry on his business.

liberté du commerce (restriction abusive à la)
undue restraint of trade

livraison
delivery
Free delivery.

> **bon de livraison**
> delivery order

> **délai de livraison**
> delivery period

> **paiement à la livraison**
> cash on delivery

> **retard de livraison**
> late delivery
> *The delivery of goods to the buyer after the date which has been agreed in the contract is called late delivery.*

location-vente
hire purchase
A hire purchase agreement.

mandat à (donner)
designate a proxy (to)
"The undersigned hereby designates as his proxy Mr X..."

mandataire
trustee
A trustee is someone who has legal control of money or property that he is keeping or investing for another person.
nominee
A nominee is a company member who holds the shares registered in his name for the benefit of another.
proxy
The undersigned hereby designates as his proxy Mr Bond.

marchandise
goods / merchandise
Goods are things that are made to be sold.

marché
market
The market is buoyant today.
bargain
A bargain is a business agreement in which two people agree what each of them will pay, do or receive.

> **arrêter un marché**
> to conclude a bargain

> **passer un marché**
> to enter into a bargain

marché à terme
settlement bargain

marché ferme
firm bargain

marque
trade mark
If a person uses a registered trade mark without the owner's permisson, the owner can sue him.

mise de fonds
outlay
An initial outlay of $5,000.

monopole
monopoly
A monopoly is the control of a particular market for goods or services by one person or a group of persons.

nantissement
collateral
A collateral is a security that is additional to the main security for a debt.

> **titres remis en nantissement**
> securities lodged as collateral

négligence
negligence
"Any claim of negligence on the part of the supplier..."

nom de (au) / pour le compte de
on behalf of
He is acting on behalf of his client.

non-révélation
non-disclosure
Non-disclosure is the failure by an insured person to disclose certain facts, which he knows or ought to know of, to the insurers.

nullité
nullity

> **frapper de nullité**
> to render void

> **nul et non avenu**
> nul and void
> *The contract was declared nul and void.*

obligation
commitment
"If such contingency occurs the Purchaser may elect (...) to buy elsewhere products to be purchased hereunder and deduct from any commitment the quantity purchased elsewhere."

> **être défaillant dans l'exécution de ses obligations**
> to fail to fulfill one's obligations

occulte
secret
Secret profit.

offre
offer
An offer is a firm proposition put by one person to another with the intention that it will become binding if accepted.

offreur / offrant
offerer

omission
omission
Omission is a failure to act.

paiement
payment
When can we expect payment?

paiement à la commande
cash with order

paiement à la livraison
cash on delivery

paiement d'avance
payment in advance

paiement échelonné
instalment

> **échelonner des paiements**
> to stagger payments

par paliers
incremental
Steady incremental increases in salary.

portée
extent
The extent of cover.

porteur
bearer
The bearer is the person who is in possession of a bearer bill.

porteur (billet au)
bearer bill
A bearer bill is a bill of exchange which has been made out so as to be payable to the bearer of that bill.

porteur (chèque au)
bearer cheque

possesseur / propriétaire
owner
A car owner.

holder
The holder is the payee or endorsee who is in possession of an order bill or bearer bill.

pouvoirs
power of attorney
A power of attorney is an authority given by one person to another to act on his behalf.

pratiques anti-concurentielles
uncompetitive practices

pratiques commerciales restrictives
restrictive trade practices
The Restrictive Practices Court deals with applications concerning restrictive trading practices.

préjudice
damage
Damage may be caused to one person's property or economic position.

prescription
lapse of time
Lapse of time is sometimes referred as laches.

présentation
presentment
A presentment is the presentation of a bill of exchange for payment.

prime
premium
A premium is the price paid by the insured person in an insurance contract in consideration for the cover he receives from the insurance company.

> **prime pour paiement comptant**
> cash payment award

prix
price
The price is the amount of money which is payable for the provision of goods or services.

> **révision de prix**
> price escalation
> *"The applicable escalation formula established by Seller is stated in Exhibit "A" of this agreement."*

prix convenu
agreed price

prix du transport
freight
The freight is the charge made by shipping companies for transport.

prix sans réserves
clean price

prix sous réserves
qualified price

procuration
proxy
"The undersigned hereby designates as his proxy Mr X or in his absence Mr Y to represent him..."

> **avoir procuration pour quelqu'un**
> be somebody's proxy
> *I am the Director's proxy at next month's company meeting.*

> **par procuration**
> by proxy

propriété
property
In English law, property is divided into real property and personal property.

reçu / récépissé
receipt
A written receipt for payment.

récépissé du transitaire
banking receipt

règlement (litige / dette)
settlement
Settlement of disputes. In full settlement.

réglementer
regulate (to)
Prices are regulated by supply and demand.

renonciation à un droit
waiver
"The failure of either party to enforce at any time any of the provisions of the Purchase Agreement (...) shall in no way be construed to be a waiver of such provisions..."

réparation
remedy
"The following remedies will apply..."

résilier
terminate (to)
"Should Seller fail to perform any of the terms and conditions of this Agreement (...) Buyer shall have the right to terminate this Agreement..."

responsabilité civile
business liability / strict liability
Business liability is the legal liability for breach of contract which may happen in the course of carrying out a business.

responsabilité conjointe et individuelle
joint and several liability

responsabilité du fabricant
manufacturer's liability

responsable
liable
They are liable only for half of their investment.

retard
delay
The delay in production.

rétention (droit de)
lien
Lien may be general or particular.

rétention de marchandises (droit de)
lien on goods
Lien is the right of an unpaid seller to retain possession of the goods until the buyer pays the price even though the property of goods has passed to the buyer.

révocation d'offre
revocation of order
A revocation of order is the withdrawal by the offerer of his offer.

risque
risk
A risk is the responsibility for loss or damage occasioned to goods.

sauvetage
salvage
Salvage is the right of an insurance company, which has paid out for a total loss of insured goods, to those goods or the value of those goods if sold.

secret de fabrication
trade secret
A trade secret is a method of production used in the course of business which is a secret of a particular manufacturer.

soumission
tender
Tenders are to be submitted on May 5th at 10 a.m.

sous-vente
sub-sale
A sub-sale is a contract of sale made by the buyer of goods with a person in contemplation of him receiving goods under the original contract with the seller.

tiré
drawee
The drawee is the party to a bill of exchange to whom an order is given to pay money to another on presentation of that document.

tireur
drawer
The party to a bill of exchange who orders money to be paid on his behalf is called the drawer.

titre
title
A title is the legal ownership in goods including the right to sell them.

titre de créance
proof / evidence of indebtness

titre de propriété
documents of title / certificate of title
A document used in business as proof of the possession or control of goods is called documents of title / certificate of title.

traite
bill of exchange
A bill of exchange is transferable and negotiable.

draft
A draft is a written order drawn by a creditor directing a debtor to pay a sum of money, usually to a bank.

traite à échéance
time draft

traite à vue
sight draft / SD

traite bancaire
banker's draft / bank draft / BD

traite documentaire
documentary bill
A documentary bill is a draft sent by the seller's bank to the purchaser's bank together with the documents concerning the goods.

transaction
bargain
The outcome of the parties' negotiations after each party has agreed to the other's consideration is called a bargain.

transférable
transferable
A bill of exchange is transferable.

> **non-transférable**
> non-transferable

transit
transit
Transit begins at the time when goods are delivered to a carrier for transmission to the buyer until the latter takes delivery from the carrier.

transport
transport / carriage / conveyance / shipping / transportation
"The seller shall select the method of transportation (...) in accordance with shipping conditions in force at the time or during the shipment."

transporteur
carrier
A carrier is someone who agrees to transport goods or passengers from one place to another.

tribunal de commerce
Commercial Court
The Commercial Court forms part of the Queen's Bench Division of the High Court.

vendable
merchantable / marketable / saleable
A merchantable quality.

> **invendable**
> unmarketable / unsaleable

vendeur
seller
The seller is the person in a contract for the sale of goods who sells or agrees to sell those goods.

> **indépendant de la volonté du vendeur**
> beyond seller's control

vente
sale
A contract by which the seller transfers the property in goods to the buyer is called a sale.

versement
payment
The payment of a sum into an account.

versement échelonné
instalment
An instalment contract.

vigueur (en)
force (in)
Patent in force at time of sale control.

> **prix en vigueur**
> current price

violation de ses engagements
breach of commitment
The alleged breach of the supplier's commitments.

DROIT DES SOCIÉTÉS
COMPANY LAW

accord (en cas de réorganisation)
scheme of arrangement
The scheme of arrangement must be voted by a 75% majority.

actif de roulement
current assets

actif et passif
assets and liabilities
If you want to buy a business, assets and liabilities have to be carefully studied.

actif immobilisé
fixed assets
In a consolidated balance-sheet you will find under the heading "fixed assets" the intangible assets, the tangible assets and the financial assets.

action
share
This company's shares have been on the way down for two years.

action convertible
convertible / common / preferred share

action nominative
registered share

action ordinaire
ordinary share / share of common stock / equity

action au porteur
bearer share

action de priorité / privilégiée
preference / preferential share / preferred stock

action sans droit de vote / certificat d'investissement
non-voting share

transfert d'actions
share transfer

actionnaire
shareholder
Shareholders are the owners of the company; they vote at the Company's General Meeting.

> **assemblée d'actionnaires**
> meeting of shareholders

> **convoquer les actionnaires**
> to summon the shareholders

administrateur
director
The board intends to increase the number of directors who will assist full time members.

trustee
Trustees remain liable for acts carried out during their trusteeship.

administrateur gérant
managing director

administrateur judiciaire
official receiver
The official receiver may have power to manage the company.

> **placer une société sous administration judiciaire**
> to call in the receiver

administrateur judiciaire (fonction d')
receivership

agent de change
stock broker
All stock brokers employ financial analysts.

aide financière
financial assistance
Financial assistance may be a loan, guarantee, security, etc., by a registered company made for the purpose of assisting somebody to acquire its shares.

amortissement
depreciation (tangible assets)
The depreciation of a machine is the decrease in value through deterioration or obsolescence; an allowance is made for this in book-keeping.
amortization (intangible assets)
writing off

année financière
financial year
The financial year ends on March 31st.

apurement des comptes
audit
They are going to conduct a full audit.

apurement d'une dette
wiping out

assemblée générale annuelle
annual general meeting / AGM
The annual general meeting is required by the Companies Act 1948.

associé
partner
He was a partner in an insurance firm.

associé commanditaire
sleeping partner

associé commandité
active partner

bénéfice
profit / earnings
He made a profit on this sale.
return
The bank is earning a huge return on our money.

> **> répartition des bénéfices**
> appropriation of profits

bénéfice des sociétés par action
company earnings

bénéfice net
net earnings

bénéfice non distribué
retained profit

bénéfice pouvant être distribué
distributable profit

bénéfices réinvestis
reinvested profits

bénéfices reportés
carried forward profits

bilan
balance-sheet
On a balance-sheet, the liabilities of business are set out on the right and the assets on the left.

> **> déposer son bilan**
> to file a petition in bankruptcy

> **> dépôt de bilan**
> statement of affairs
> *A statement of affairs is a document that gives details of the debtor's assets, debts and liabilities, the names and addresses of his creditors, and what securities they hold.*

bilan consolidé
consolidated balance

> **> présentation fallacieuse du bilan**
> window-dressing

bilan d'ouverture de liquidation
statement of affairs
A statement of affairs is a document that must be prepared by a debtor after a receiving order has been made against him.

Bourse
Stock Exchange
In most papers, you find the Stock Exchange report.

> **> entrer à la Bourse (s'introduire)**
> to go public / to be listed on the Stock Exchange.

capital
capital
You can gain control of a business by putting up most of the capital.

capital (dans société par actions)
capital action / capital stock

capital autorisé
authorized / nominal capital
Authorized / Nominal capital is the total value of the shares that a registered com-

pany is authorized to issue in order to raise capital.

capital entièrement libéré
capital entirely paid up
According to the French law concerning the limited liability companies, the capital must be entirely paid up in 5 years.

capital social
registered capital / authorized capital

capitaux permanents
invested capital / capital base / capital accounts / capital employed
Capital account is the sum of capital base and long term debts.

caution (bancaire)
guarantee / security / surety / bond
"Supplier shall furnish such performance bond or other security, at the time, in such a form, issued by such surety (bank or insurance company) and in the amount Customer may require or approve pursuant to other provisions of the agreement."

certificat d'actions
share certificate
A share certificate is a document certifying that a person is a company member and stating the number of shares registered in his name.

cessation de paiement
act of bankruptcy
The bankruptcy petition must usually show that the debtor has committed an act of bankruptcy.

cession (acte de transfert)
assignation

cession d'actions
transfer of shares
Transfer of shares is a process by which the rights and liabilities in a share are transferred from one person to another.

chiffre d'affaires
turnover
The annual turnover of this firm was $10 billion in 1991.

commissaire aux comptes
auditor
The auditor came to certify that all legal transactions had been honest and legal.

> **rapport des commissaires aux comptes**
> report of auditors

comptabilité
accountancy / book-keeping
He made a brilliant career in accountancy / book-keeping.

comptable
accountant
This accountant provides the best advice available.

> **expert-comptable**
> chartered accountant
> *The accounts of a company are checked every year by a chartered accountant.*

compte
account
A bank account.

> **arrêté de compte**
> ruling of account

> **compte arrêté**
> ruled off / settled account

> **livre de comptes (registre)**
> books of account
> *Books of account are records that disclose a company's financial position.*

compte courant
running account

compte d'exploitation
operating account / trading statement / trading account

compte de pertes et profits
statement of earnings

compte de résultat
revenue account

conciliateur
arbitrator
Arbitrators may adopt whatever procedure they choose.

constitution en société
incorporation / registration
Incorporation / Registration is the method by which a company comes into existence.

> **non constitué**
> unincorporated
> *An unincorporated association is a body consisting of a number of persons who have come together in pursuance of a common interest, e.g. a sports club.*

coté
listed
Listed securities.

> **non coté**
> unlisted

courtier
cf. « agent de change »

créance
debt
A debt is a sum of money owed by one person for services rendered by another person.

créance douteuse
bad debt

créance irrécouvrable
irrecoverable debt

créancier
creditor
Like any other creditor, the bank may sue for its money.

créancier chirographaire
unsecured creditor
An unsecured creditor has lent money without getting any security.

créancier nanti
secured creditor
A secured creditor holds some security for money he has lent.

créancier privilégié
preferential creditor
A preferential creditor has priority of payment.

créancier titulaire d'une créance exécutoire issue d'un jugement
judgment creditor
A judgment creditor is someone in whose favour a court judgment is made against a debtor.

débiteur
debtor
A debtor is a person who owes money.

détournement de fonds
embezzlement / misappropriation
This charge of embezzlement is sheer slander.

dette
debt
You should spend less money until your debts are paid off.

> **échéance d'une dette**
> maturity of a debt

dettes à court terme
current liabilities

dettes à long et moyen terme
deferred liabilities / fixed liabilities / long and medium liabilities

directeur
manager (banque, entreprise)
director (administrateur, propriétaire)
The board intends to increase the number of directors who will assist full time members.

directeur fictif
shadow director

directeur général
general manager / president (US)

diriger une affaire
manage (to) / run a company (to)
Our boss has been running / managing the company for 20 years.

dissolution
dissolution
Dissolution is the dissolving of a company.

dividende
dividend
Fictitious dividend.

endettement
liabilities
cf. « dette »

exercice social
accounting year / financial year
The financial year ends on March 31st.

> **produit de l'exercice**
> return of the year

failli
bankrupt
To declare a debtor to be bankrupt, a creditor must file a bankruptcy petition.

> **en faillite personnelle (personne)**
> undischarged bankrupt
> *An undischarged bankrupt is disqualified from holding certain offices.*

falsifié
forged
I think someone has forged my signature.

fermer définitivement (entreprise)
close down (to)
I am afraid we'll be forced to close down our factory by the end of the year.

fictif
fictitious / sham
Fictitious assets.

filiale
subsidiary
IBM has foreign subsidiaries all over the world.

flux de trésorerie
cash flow
Cash flow statement.

fondateur
promoter/ founder
A promoter is someone who floats a company, who takes the initiative of forming it.

fonds
funds
Public funds.

fonds de roulement
working capital

fonds propres
proprietorship / ownership

frais
expenses
Extra expenses.

frais d'exploitation
operating costs / working expenses

frais généraux
overhead expenses / costs / oncosts charges / standing expenses

fraude
fraud
Prevention of Frauds Act 1958.

frauduleux
fraudulent
A fraudulent balance-sheet.

> **moyens frauduleux**
> fraudulent means

fusion
merger / amalgamation
When two companies combine their assets it is called a merger.

> **sociétés fusionnées**
> amalgamated companies

fusionner
merge (to)

garant
guarantor
The guarantor is sometimes referred to as a security.

garantie
cf. « caution »

garantir
guarantee (to)

gérer (une affaire)
manage / run / conduct (to)
After her father's death, she decided to manage the firm by herself.

gestion
management
A diploma in business and management.

> **mauvaise gestion**
> mismanagement / misconduct

immobilisations
fixed assets
In a consolidated balance-sheet, you will find under the heading "fixed assets" the intangible assets, the tangible assets and the financial assets.

impôt sur les sociétés
corporate tax
Company managers consider that the corporate tax acts as a brake upon investments.

insolvabilité
insolvency

insolvable
insolvent
A person who is insolvent does not have enough money to pay his debts.

investissement initial
outlay
An outlay is an amount of money that is invested in a business.

liquidateur
liquidator
cf « administrateur judiciaire »
The process of winding up involves the appointment of a liquidator who collects the assets and pays debts.

liquidation
liquidation / winding up
The firm faced liquidation / winding up in 1990.

> **valeur de liquidation**
> realization value

liquidation d'actifs
administration of assets

liquidation des opérations
closing

liquidation d'un compte
settlement

liquidation d'une affaire
realization

liquidation forcée
compulsory winding up

liquidation volontaire
voluntary winding up

liquider une affaire
wind up a business (to)

maison mère
parent company
ITT is a parent company which owns a lot of subsidiaries in the US and abroad.

mandataire
proxy
"The undersigned hereby designates as his proxy Mr X to represent him..."

monopole
monopoly
A monopoly of an industry is control of most of the industry by only one or a few large firms.

multinationale
multinational company
Unilever is an important multinational corporation which produces and sells products in a lot of countries.

nationalisé
state-owned / nationalised
The BBC has been a state-owned / nationalised company since 1927.

nom de société
business name
The choice of a business name is restricted by the Companies Act 1981.

objet
objects clause
The memorandum of association states the purpose for which the company was formed, this is called the objects clause.

obligation
cf « dette »

obligation (titre)
debenture (US) / bond (GB)
If a government wants to raise money for public investment, it issues bonds.

obligation de gestion intelligente
obligation of care and skill

ordonnance de mise sous séquestre
receiving order
A receiving order is a court order made during the course of bankruptcy proceedings that places the debtor's property under the control of the official receiver.

ordonnance de saisie et de mise en liquidation des biens du condamné
criminal bankruptcy order

partage d'actions
allotment
An allotment gives an applicant for shares the unconditional right to purchase a specified number of shares.

PDG
chairman and managing director
The company's former chairman and managing director.

personnalité morale (obtention de)
corporation
A corporation has legal personality, it may be a corporation sole or a corporation aggregate.

> **certificat d'obtention de la personnalité morale**
> certificate of incorporation
> *The certificate of incorporation is given by the registrar.*

préemption (droit de)
pre-emptive right
The pre-emptive right is the right of some shareholders to be offered a proportion of certain classes of newly issued securities before they are offered to others.

président du conseil d'administration
chairman of the board
The chairman of the board is the nominal head of the company.

prise de contrôle
take-over
A merchant bank handles company takeovers.

> **comité de surveillance des prises de contrôle et des fusions**
> panel on take-overs and mergers

profit
net profit (GB et US) / net income (US) / earnings
He made a $1000 net profit on this sale.

référé (procédure)
summary proceedings

registre des actionnaires
register
Shareholders' names are recorded on the register of members.

registre des sociétés
Companies registry

règlement judiciaire
bankruptcy / business failure
Bankruptcy is the state of a person who has been adjudged by a court to be insolvent.

réhabilitation d'un failli
discharge
After discharge, the debtor is freed from most of the disabilities to which he was subject.

relevé
statement
A bank statement.

rendement
return / yield
Before you make an investment decision, you should consider the risk and the return.

rentabilité
profitability
The high profitability of this business.

report sur les années antérieures
carryback
Losses carryback.

report sur les années futures
carryforward

requête des créanciers
petition in bankruptcy
To declare a debtor to be bankrupt, a creditor must make an application to the High

Court or to a county court, this application is known as a bankruptcy petition.

résolution spéciale
special resolution
All the clauses of the articles and most of those of the memorandum can be amended by a special resolution.

responsabilité
liability
When you have liability for a debt, you are legally responsible for it.

> **solidairement responsable**
> jointly and severally responsible

secrétaire général
company secretary
The company secretary keeps the company's statutory books.

siège
headquarters / head office
The managing director's office is situated in the company's headquarters / head office.

siège social
head office

société
company
An oil company.

> **constitution d'une société**
> flotation

> **constitution en société**
> incorporation
> *An incorporation is the formation of an association that has legal capacity.*

> **fonder une société**
> to float a company
> *A promoter is a person who floats a company.*

> **se constituer en société**
> to incorporate
> *When a company is incorporated, it has its own rights and liabilities.*

société anonyme (équivalent)
public company (GB) / private corporation (US)

société contrôlée à hauteur de 20 %
associated company (GB)

société dont le capital est divisé en actions négotiables mais dont les actionnaires ont une responsabilité illimitée
joint stock company (US)

société du groupe
affiliated company (GB)

société nationalisée
public corporation (GB)

société nationalisée / entreprise publique
public corporation (US: contrôlée par le gouvernement ou une municipalité)

société par actions
limited liability company (GB) / incorporated company (GB) / joint stock company (structure différente selon GB ou US) / private company (GB) / private corporation (US : société où les actionnaires sont des organismes ou personnes privées)

société semblable à une SARL
Limited liability partnership (GB)

solde
balance
We demand payment of the balance within a week.

solde créditeur
favorable balance

solde débiteur
adverse balance

solvable
solvent
If a person or a company is solvent, they have enough money to pay all their debts.

statuts
articles of association
The articles of association are drawn up when a company is set up.

syndic de faillite
receiver
An official receiver is a person appointed by the Department of Trade who acts in bankruptcy matters as interim receiver and manager of the estate of the debtor.

tribunal de commerce
Commercial Court
The Commercial Court forms part of the Queen's Bench Division.

vérification
inspection and investigation of a company
An inspection and investigation of a company is an inquiry into the running of a company made by inspectors who are appointed by the Department of Trade.

DROIT FISCAL

TAX LAW

abattement
allowance
The amount of tax based on a person's total income for the year less certain allowances.

allègement fiscal
tax relief
There exist certain agreements with a lot of countries to give tax relief against double taxation.

amortissement admis par le fisc
capital allowance
Capital allowance is a tax allowance for business on capital expenditure, on machinery, industrial buildings, etc.

arrérages
arrears
Arrears are amounts of money that you owe.

assiette de l'impôt
tax assessment basis / tax base
The income is the tax assessment basis for the income tax.

assujettissement à l'impôt
liability to tax
Tax avoidance is planning one's affairs so as to reduce liability to tax.

avoir fiscal
tax credit
Tax credit cushions tax duplication on the profits which are distributed to shareholders.

barème des impôts
tax scale / tax rate
A degressive tax scale.

budget
budget
Each year the Chancellor of the Exchequer presents a budget to Parliament.

cédule
schedule
The types of taxable income are set out in the Income and Corporation Taxes Act 1970 under six schedules.

charge fiscale
tax burden

commissaire aux affaires générales des impôts
Commissioner for the General Purposes of the Income Tax
The Commissioners for the General Purposes of the Income Tax are better known as General Commissioners.

commissaire aux Douanes et à la Régie
Commissioner for Customs and Excise

commissaire des Contributions directes
Commissioner for HM Revenue and Customs

conseiller fiscal
tax consultant / tax preparer
You should have contacted a firm of tax consultants before, they would have been able to help you to make out your tax return.

contribuable
tax payer
As usual the tax payer will have to foot the bill.

contrôleur des Contributions directes
tax inspector / inspector of taxes
Inspector of taxes are responsible for assessing taxes.

déclaration de revenus
income tax return
In France, you must send your income tax return each year in May.

> **déductible des impôts**
tax deductible
In France, charitable contributions and interest payments are tax deductible up to a certain amount.

> **ne pas déclarer**
not to report

> **ne pas déclarer en totalité**
to skim one's income

> **truquer sa déclaration**
to fiddle / to cook one's income tax return

déductions avant impôts
tax allowances
On your tax sheet you put down all your income from whatever source, then you put down your allowable deductions; those deductions are called tax allowances.

déduction pour dons
deduction for donations

déduction pour frais professionnels
deductions for expenses

dégrèvement d'impôts
tax relief
If HM Revenue and Customs has taxed you too much, it can return a tax relief to you.

détermination du montant de l'impôt
assessment
Tax inspectors are responsible for the assessment of taxes.

double imposition
tax duplication
Tax duplication can be avoided thanks to tax credit.

droits de succession
inheritance tax

droits de timbre
stamp duty
Stamp duty payable by the seller.

évasion fiscale
tax evasion / tax dodging / tax avoidance
Concealing or failing to declare income is tax evasion.

exonération fiscale
tax exemption

exonéré d'impôts
tax-exempt
Those bonds are tax-exempt.

feuille d'impôts
tax sheet / tax return
Don't forget to send your tax sheet / tax return by May 31st.

fisc
HM Revenue and Customs
(HMRC / Her Majesty's Revenue and Customs)
The income tax is paid to HM Revenue and Customs.

fiscale (année)
fiscal / tax year

fraude fiscale
tax evasion / tax dodging / tax avoidance
Tax avoidance / dodging / evasion consists in avoiding the lawful assessment of taxes.

imposable
taxable
Taxable goods.

imposition
taxation
The Prime Minister is hoping to reduce taxation.

> **base d'imposition**
taxable base

impôt foncier
land /property tax
Land owners generally have to pay land taxes.

impôt par individu
poll tax

impôt prélevé à la source
PAYE / Pay As You Earn
In Great Britain, the income tax is deducted and paid by employers on behalf of their employees; it is called PAYE.

impôt sur le capital
capital tax
Capital taxes include estate duty, capital gains tax and the tax on short-term gains.

impôt sur le revenu
income tax

impôt sur le revenu commercial
business income tax

impôt sur les plus-values
capital gains tax
If your shares have increased beyond a certain percentage and if you decide to sell them, you will have to pay capital gains tax.

impôt sur les sociétés
corporation tax

impôt sur les successions
inheritance tax

impôt sur les traitements et salaires
employment income tax

impôt sur le transfert de capitaux
capital transfer tax / CTT

impôts déduits
less tax
Interest less tax.

impôts directs
direct taxes
In France, the income tax belongs to the direct taxes.

impôts indirects
excise duties / taxes
Taxes on expenditure include customs and excise duties taxes.

impôts locaux
local rates
Local rates can be very heavy in certain areas.

impôts non déclarés
unreported tax

impôts sous évalués
understated / underevalued / underreported tax

paradis fiscal
tax heaven / tax shelter
Monaco is a tax heaven / shelter.

percepteur
tax collector
A tax collector is a civil servant whose job is to collect different sorts of taxes.

prélèvement libératoire / forfaitaire
standard deduction

progressif
progressive
A progressive tax has a higher rate for persons with higher incomes.

proportionnel
proportional
A proportional tax has the same percentage of each person's income whether rich or poor.

recette des impôts
yield from tax

reste (ce qu'il reste après impôt)
after tax retention

retenue à la source
withholding tax

revenu
income
Your income is the money you earn or you get from other sources such as investments for instance.

revenu des placements / investissements
investment income

revenu disponible
discretionary income

revenu imposable
taxable income / assessed income

revenu légal
statutory income

revenu total
total income

Service de la répression des fraudes
Fraud Squad
The Fraud Squad is a section of the police force that is responsible for dealing with fraud.

soumis à l'impôt
taxable / dutiable / liable to tax
If something is taxable, you have to pay tax on it.

taux de base
basic rate
Certain incomes are exempt from the basic rate.

taux d'imposition
tax rate

taxe à la valeur ajoutée / TVA
value-added tax / VAT
Exclusive of VAT.

tranche d'imposition
tax bracket / tax band
The system of progressive taxes has got scales with several tax brackets / bands.

> **répartir par tranche**
> to band a tax

Trésor public
Treasury
The Treasury is the financial aspect of administrative power.

DROIT DU TRAVAIL
LABOUR LAW

accident du travail
industrial injury
An industrial injury is an injury sustained in the course of employment.

> **assurance accident du travail**
> employers' liability insurance

> **indemnité d'accident du travail**
> industrial injury benefit
> *Industrial injury benefit is payable only while the employee remains incapable of work and for a maximum of 26 weeks.*

> **loi sur les accidents du travail**
> Factory Act / Workmen's Compensation Act

accord
agreement
The employees managed to come to an agreement with their boss.

arbitrage
arbitration
Arbitration between employers and trade unions.

arbitrage en cas de grève
strike arbitration

arbitrage en matière de salaire
wage arbitration

avantages
benefits
Employee benefits can be split into four groups: deferred income and income replacement; leave, redundancy and retirement; financial; and good-will.

avantages en espèces
cash benefits

avantages en nature
benefits in kind

avantages supplémentaires
fringe benefits

avertissement
warning of dismissal
A warning of dismissal is a process by which an employee is given a warning that, if his conduct or performance do not improve, he is liable to be dismissed.

capital décès
industrial death benefit
Industrial death benefit is a state pension payable to the widow of a man who has died from injuries sustained in the course of his employment.

certificat de travail
attestation of employment
I have not been given my attestation of employment.

chômage
unemployment
An increase in unemployment figures.

chômage (être au)
jobless / workless / unemployed (to be)
Those miners have been jobless / workless / unemployed for two years now.

on the dole (to be)
Someone who is on the dole receives money regularly from the government.

> **allocation chômage**
> unemployment benefit
> *Unemployment benefit payable under the Social Security Act 1975.*

> **assurance chômage**
> compulsory unemployment insurance

> **fonds d'assurance chômage**
> unemployment fund

> **indemnité chômage**
> unemployment dole

> **mettre au chômage technique**
to lay off
If a factory is out of raw materials (because of a strike for instance),the workers in the factory can be laid off.

> **taux de chômage**
jobless rate/ unemployment rate
The jobless rate / unemployment rate is getting more and more disturbing.

> **travailleurs mis au chômage technique**
lay-offs

chômage de longue durée
long-term unemployment
Long-term unemployment is less important in the States than in Europe.

chômage partiel
unemployment on short time / short-time working
We'll have to put a few employees on short-time working.

chômage structurel
structural unemployment
An important part of underemployment of unskilled workers can be called structural unemployment.

comité central d'arbitrage
Central Arbitration Committee / CAC
The Central Arbitration Committee was established under the Employment Protection Act 1975.

comité d'entreprise
works committee

conciliation
conciliation
Conciliation officers.

conflit du travail
industrial conflict / trade dispute / labour dispute
Industrial conflict / Trade dispute / Labour dispute is any dispute between workers and their employer relating to terms and conditions of employment for example.

congé
leave
A 48 hours' leave.

congé annuel
annual leave

congé à salaire plein
full-pay leave

congé de maternité
maternity leave

congé de maternité rémunéré
maternity pay

congé maladie
sick leave

congés payés
holidays with pay / paid holiday

congé sans traitement
unpaid leave

congédier
dismiss (to)
The R&D manager has been dismissed.

conseil des prud'hommes
industrial tribunal
An industrial tribunal hears complaints concerning unfair dismissal, redundancy, equal pay and maternity rights.

contrat de travail
contract of employment
In every contract of employment a duty of mutual confidence and trust is implied.

convention collective
collective agreement
A collective agreement is an agreement between trade union and employer resulting from collective bargaining.

délégué du personnel / délégué syndical
shop steward
A shop steward is a trade union member who is elected by the other members in a factory or office to speak for them at official meetings.

démission
resignation
My employer has accepted my resignation.

démissionner
resign (to)

discrimination
discrimination
The Sex Discrimination Act 1975.

devoirs syndicaux
union duties
An employee who is a trade union official is entitled to time off work for official union duties.

dommages et intérêts
damages
Damages are granted by a court as compensation for a breach of contract for example.

droits
rights
Trade unions' negotiating rights.

égalité des salaires
equal pay
The Equal Pay Act 1970.

> **clause d'égalité**
> equality clause
> *Equality clause is a clause in a contract of employment for a woman stipulating that if she has the same employment as a man, the terms of the contract must place her in no less favourable a position than a man.*

embaucher
hire / take on (to)
An employer often hires / takes on women because they are cheaper.

émeute
riot
The Riot Act 1886.

émoluments
emoluments
Emoluments are a person's earnings including salaries, fees, wages and profits.

emploi
employment
An employment agency.

employé
employee
The employee claimed he had been dismissed without notice.

employeur
employer
This plant is a major employer in the area.

essai (période d')
probation period
He is still in his probation period.

faute professionnelle
professional misconduct
He was dismissed for professional misconduct.

faute professionnelle lourde
gross professional misconduct

fiche de paye détaillée
itemized pay statement / itemized pay slip
An itemized pay slip / statement is a written statement with which an employer must provide an employee each time his salary is paid to him.

formation (plan de)
training scheme
This training scheme proved to be a sheer failure.

formation professionnelle
vocational training
This college is specialized in vocational training.

grève
strike
The airline pilots are on strike again.

> **allocation de grève**
> strike pay
> *Strike pay is money which is paid to workers who are on strike.*

> **être en grève**
> to be on strike

> **piquet de grève**
> picketing
> *Mass picketing.*

> **se mettre en grève**
> to go on strike
> *The shop steward announced that the workers had decided to go on strike.*

grève avec occupation d'usine
stay-in strike

grève de solidarité
sympathetic strike

grève du zèle
work-to-rule strike

grève perlée
go-slow strike

grève sauvage
wildcat strike

grève surprise
snap strike / lightning strike

grève totale
all-out strike

gréviste
striker
The strikers wanted better working conditions.

handicapé
disabled person
Under the Disabled Persons Employment Act 1944, every employer of 20 or more people is obliged to employ a quota of disabled persons.

harcèlement
harassment
What is psychological harassment in the work place?

heures de travail
schedule
Flexitime would considerably alter schedules in our firm.

heures supplémentaires
overtime
From now on, the employees will refuse to work overtime.

horaires variables
flexitime / variable work schedules / alternative work schedules / variable working hours
Life has been considerably easier since I started being on flexitime.

indemnité de licenciement
dismissal payment / redundancy pay / severance pay
Redundancy pay / Severance pay is the sum of money that an employee dismissed because of redundancy is entitled to receive from his employer.

inspecteur du travail
factory inspector
The factory inspector visited the workshop yesterday.

invalidité
disability
The disabilities suffered by the miners.

> **pension d'invalidité**
> industrial disablement benefit
> *Industrial disablement benefit is a lump sum payable by the State to a person disabled by injury suffered in the course of his employment.*

invalidité permanente
chronic ill health

jour férié
bank holiday
Bank holidays are days that are declared holidays under the Banking and Financial Dealing Act 1971.

jour ouvrable
working day
A working day is any day other than Saturday, Sunday and bank holidays.

licenciement
dismissal
The dismissal of the accounts manager was discussed for a few days.

licenciement (préavis de)
term of notice

licenciement abusif
unfair dismissal
Unfair dismissal is the dismissal of an employee that the employer cannot prove to be fair.

licenciement fautif
wrongful dismissal

licenciement justifié
fair dismissal

maladie
sickness
They are not working, is it because of sickness or unemployment?

> **assurance maladie**
> health insurance

> **caisse de maladie**
> sick-benefit insurance

> **congé de maladie**
> cf. « congé »

> **prestation-maladie**
> sick-benefit
> *Sick-benefit is money that a person receives regularly from the government when he is unable to work because of illness.*

maladie professionnelle
industrial disease

maternité
maternity
Maternity rights.

> **allocation de maternité**
> maternity allowances

monopole syndical d'embauche
closed shop
A closed shop is a factory or business in which employees must be members of a particular trade union.

négotiation collective
collective bargaining
Negotiations between trade unions and employers about terms and conditions of employment are called collective bargaining.

participation
industrial democracy
Industrial democracy is participation in company management by employees.

participation aux résultats de l'entreprise
profit-sharing scheme
Profit-sharing scheme is a system by which all the employees in a company have a share in its benefits.

patron
employer / boss (fam.)
Your employer / boss is the person you work for.

patronat
employers

> **association patronale**
> employers' association
> *Under the Trade Union and Labour Relations Act 1974, employers' association have the same legal status as trade unions.*

pension
pension
An old age pension.

pension de retraite
retiring pension / allowance / pay

pension d'invalidité
invalid pension / industrial disablement benefit

personnel
staff, personnel
"Staff only."
The personnel Manager.

préavis (délai de)
notice period

> **sans préavis**
> without notice

préavis de licenciement
notice
An employee dismissed without due notice can claim damages in the courts for wrongful dismissal.

prestations sociales
social insurance benefits
You are entitled to social insurance benefits.

prime
incentive
Incentive wages.

prime d'ancienneté
seniority pay

prime de licenciement
severance pay

prime d'encouragement
incentive bonus

prime de vie chère
cost of living allowance

prime pour travail de nuit
night work bonus

raison légitime
good reason

> **sans raison légitime**
> without good reason
> *A worker cannot be dismissed without good reason.*

réintégration dans l'entreprise
re-engagement order
A re-engagement order is an order made by an industrial tribunal directing an employer who has unfairly dismissed an employee to provide him with comparable employment from that from which he was dismissed.

reinstatement order
A reinstatement order is an order made by an industrial tribunal directing an employer who has unfairly dismissed an employee to restore him to his former job.

renvoi
cf « licenciement »

retenue
deduction
Deduction from a pension scheme.

> **faire une retenue sur le salaire**
> to deduct from the wages
> *In Great Britain the income tax is deducted from the wages and paid by employers on behalf of their employees.*

> **faire une retenue de X sur le salaire de qqn**
> to stop X out of someone's wages

retraite
retirement
Since his retirement his health has been considerably improving.

> **caisse de retraite**
> pension fund / superannuation fund
> *The firm has been operating its own superannuation fund / pension fund for a few years.*

salaire
pay
Your pay is the money you are given as your wages or salary.
salary (cadres et employés)
The salary of our new sales manager will depend on his previous experience.

wage / wages (travailleurs manuels et non qualifiés)
This family lives on a low wage / low wages.

> **échelle mobile des salaires**
> sliding wage scale

> **salaire brut**
> gross wage

> **salaire minimum interprofessionnel garanti**
> guaranteed minimum wage
> *In France the guaranteed minimum wage is renewed at least once a year.*

> **salaire net**
> net wage

sécurité
safety
Safety at work.

> **comité d'hygiène, de sécurité et des conditions de travail / CHSCT**
> safety committee
> *A safety committee is a committee that an employer must establish within three months after a written request from at least two employees' safety representatives.*

somme forfaitaire
lump sum
A lump sum is paid to a worker when his degree of disablement is assessed at less than 20%.

syndicat
trade union
Why should we join a trade union?

syndical (délégué)
shop steward / trade union official
An employee who is a shop steward / trade union official is entitled to time off work for certain union purposes.

> **cotisation syndicale**
> union duty / union dues

travail au noir
moonlighting
Moonlighting was once thought to be a temporary phenomenon made necessary by the ravages of inflation.

travail posté
shiftwork
Shiftwork is widespread in iron and steel industry.

travail temporaire
temporary work
Temporary work offers a lot of advantages for the employer.

tribunal d'appel
Employment Appeal Tribunal / EAT
The Employment Appeal Tribunal / EAT is a statutory body established to hear appeals from industrial tribunals.

DROIT DE LA FAMILLE

FAMILY LAW

abandon du domicile conjugal
desertion
Desertion is the failure by a husband or wife to cohabit with his / her spouse.

adoption
adoption
The Registrar General must keep a register containing details of all adoption orders.

adoptif
adoptive
An adoptive father.

adultère
adultery
Adultery may be evidence of breakdown of marriage.

autorité locale
local authority
Local authorities have various duties in relation to the welfare of minors.

bâtard
bastard
A bastard may become legitimate by the process of legitimation.

battue (femme)
battered wife
A battered wife is a woman subjected to physical violence by her husband.

biens du ménage
household goods
Third Report on Family Property: the Matrimonial Home and Household Goods.

biens mobiliers
movable property

biens personnels
personal property

bigamie
bigamy
Bigamy is a crime, punishable by up to 7 years' imprisonment.

brisé (mariage)
broken down
"The marriage has been broken down irretrievably."

cohabiter
cohabit (to)
The duty to cohabit.

concubinage
common-law marriage / commonlaw couple
Common-law marriage is the situation of two unmarried people living together as husband and wife.

conjoint(e)
spouse
A marriage settlement provides an income for one spouse or the children, while securing the capital for the other spouse.

conjoint fautif
offending spouse

consommation (du mariage)
consummation
Consumation of a marriage is its completion by an act of sexual intercourse.

> **non-consommation**
> non-consummation
> *Non-consummation is a ground for nullity of marriage.*

déclaration de naissance
registration of birth
The Births and Deaths Registration Act 1953.

défunt (nom)
deceased (the)
The property of the deceased.

devoirs parentaux
parental duties
Parental duties consist for the parents in maintaining and educating their children.

dissolution (du mariage)
dissolution
Dissolution is the legal termination of a marriage

divorce
divorce
Divorce Reform Act 1969.

> **cause de divorce**
> ground for divorce

> **demande en divorce**
> petition for divorce

> **demander le divorce**
> to file a petition for divorce

> **divorce par consentement mutuel**
> divorce by mutual consent

> **ordonnance de divorce**
> cf « ordonnance »

divorce (procédure de)
divorce proceedings

> **tribunal de grande instance (divorce)**
> Divorce Registry
> *The Divorce Registry is the section of the Family Division having jurisdiction over divorce proceedings.*

domicile conjugal
matrimonial home
Matrimonial home is the home in which husband and wife live together.

> **abandon du domicile conjugal**
> desertion
> *Desertion may be evidence of breakdown of marriage.*

droits parentaux
parental rights
Parents have parental rights over their children.

enfant
child
Employment of Children Act 1973.

enfant (intérêt de l')
child welfare

enfant illégitime
illegitimate child
The mother of an illegitimate child has exclusive rights to its custody.

enfant naturel
natural child
A natural child is an illegitimate child.

époux, épouse
spouse
A deserted spouse.

garde (droit de)
custody / custodianship
The Children Act 1975 distinguishes between legal custody and actual custody.

> **accorder le droit de garde**
> to grant custody

> **droit de garde effectif**
> actual custody

> **droit de garde juridique**
> legal custody

grossesse
pregnancy
Abortion is the termination of a pregnancy at a stage when the foetus is incapable of independent survival.

jugement en constatation de paternité
affiliation order
Failure to comply with the terms of an affiliation order may be punished by committal to prison.

légitime
legitimate
A legitimate child.

légitimité
legitimacy
Legitimacy Act 1976.

majorité
majority / full age
The age of majority was originally 21 years.

mariage
marriage
A marriage ceremony.

> **acte de mariage**
mariage certificate

> **mariage blanc**
sham marriage
A sham marriage is a marriage entered into for some ulterior motive, without the intention of cohabiting with the other spouse.

maternité
maternity
Maternity rights.

matrimonial
matrimonial
Matrimonial proceedings.

mineur
infant / minor
Guardianship of Minors Act 1971.

naissance
birth
A birth certificate.

nul
nul / void

nullité du mariage
nullity
The grounds for nullity are for instance lack of age, lack of consent, non-consumation, etc.

obligation alimentaire
maintenance
Maintenance is also known as financial provision or financial relief.

obligation des parents
parental duties

ordonnance
order
An order is a direction or command of a court.

ordonnance d'adoption
adoption order

ordonnance d'assistance
care order

ordonnance de divorce
decree of divorce

ordonnance de garde
custodianship order

ordonnance de garde conjointe
split order
A split order grants legal custody to one parent and care and control to the other.

ordonnance de séparation
judicial separation order
A judicial separation order is an order by the courts that a husband and wife do not have to cohabit.

PACS
contract of civil union
In France the contract of civil union or PACS has been in force since November 1999.

parent
parent
Parents have parental rights over their children.

parents adoptifs
adoptive parents

parents naturels
natural parents
After adoption, the natural parents are no longer considered in law to be the parents of the child.

parents nourriciers
foster parents
Foster parents have no legal rights over the children they foster.

paternité
paternity
He acknowledged his paternity of Jennifer's child.

paternité (action en recherche de)
paternity suit

paternité judiciaire (reconnaissance de)
affiliation order
Failure to comply with the terms of an affiliation order may be punished by committal to prison.

pension alimentaire
maintenance / financial relief / financial allowance / financial provision
Maintenance is the obligation after a divorce of one spouse to support another or of a parent to support a child of the family.

> **réclamer une pension alimentaire auprès de**
> to claim maintenance through

polygamie
polygamy
Polygamy is the practice of having more than one spouse.

procédure de prise en charge
care proceedings
Care proceedings may be taken if a child is ill-treated.

procédure en matière familiale
domestic proceedings

proche parenté (de)
closely related

protection de l'enfant
child care
Child Care Act 1980.

pupille
ward
The ward was committed to the care of a local authority.

putatif
putative
A man alleged to be the father of an illegitimate child is a putative father.

reconnaissance
legitimation
Legitimation is the process of replacing the status of illegitimacy by that of legitimacy.

reconnaître
legitimate (to)
A child may be legitimated if his parents marry one another.

relations sexuelles
sexual intercourse
Consummation of marriage is the completion of marriage by an act of sexual intercourse.

responsabilité
liability
Parents' liability.

responsable
liable
Parents may be liable for their own negligence in failing to supervise young children.

saisie-arrêt sur salaire (décision de)
attachment of earnings order
In an attachment of earnings order payment is usually in instalments.

séparation
separation
A judicial separation order.

sévices exercés sur un enfant
child abuse
Child abuse is molestation of children by parents or others.

tutelle
wardship
Wardship proceedings are heard in private.

> **sous tutelle**
> in ward / under the care of

tuteur
guardian
The parents of a child are its natural guardians.

visite (droit de)
access
Access is the opportunity to visit a child that is granted to its parent after divorce.

INDEX FRANÇAIS

A

B

D

E

F

G

H

I

P

Q

R

S

INDEX ANGLAIS

B

C

D

E

F

G

H

I

J

K

L

M

N

O

P

Q

R

T

U

V